ARTISTS

OF CAPE ANN

A 150 YEAR TRADITION

First published in the United States by:
Twin Lights Publishers, Inc.
10 Hale Street
Rockport, Massachusetts 01966
Telephone: (978) 546-7398
http://www.twinlightspub.com

ISBN 1-885435-18-5

10 9 8 7 6 5 4 3 2

Frontispiece:
Sailing Out of Gloucester
WINSLOW HOMER
1880 WATERCOLOR ON PAPER 13" X 19"
COLLECTION OF CANAJOHARIE LIBRARY
AND ART GALLERY

Front Cover:
Man in a Boat
WILLIAM LAMB PICKNELL
CA. 1883 - 1891 OIL ON CANVAS 29 1/2" X 39 1/2"
PHOTO COURTESY OF THE WILLIAM LAMB PICKNELL
CATALOGUE RAISONNE PROJECT

Book Design by:
SYP Design & Production
www.sypdesign.com

Printed in China

THE BIGGEST surprise I had in working on this book was that such a book did not already exist. Of the many art colonies that have emerged in America—Old Lyme, New Hope, Woodstock, the Hoosier School, Taos, Provincetown, Laguna, Ogunquit and Cornish—virtually all have been the subject of art books that define the significant members and present examples of their work. All have been the subject of such books except Cape Ann—the oldest, most continuously active art colony in America.

Such regionally-focused art books are usually the barometer by which one measures the importance of a colony or a style in a larger art history context. But Cape Ann's 150 year contribution to an American artistic identity is much greater than would be suggested by a quick browse through the art history section of a bookstore. Indeed, such a book is long overdue.

Many painters who worked on Cape Ann have been the subject of independent studies or exhibitions. Fitz Hugh Lane, Winslow Homer, Stuart Davis, Frederick Mulhaupt and many others have been featured in books or catalogues covering their individual body of work created on or inspired by Cape Ann.

The selection of artists to be included in this book was, of course, a tricky process. Indeed, those readers familiar with Cape Ann art who have their favorites may be puzzled by the presence of certain painters and bewildered by the absence of others. The original list of artists considered was far too long, therefore, a broad impression has been attempted, beginning with Fitz Hugh Lane, followed by the Luminists and other artists of the Hudson River era, Tonalism through Impressionism, Post-Impressionism, the Ashcan School and the Modernists.

Some painters, like Hassam and Hopper are national icons. Their presence adds prestige to the legacy of the region, and one often discovers that their visits to Cape Ann had a profound change on their work. Other painters, like George W. Harvey and William Lester Stevens have been included because of their importance as gifted homegrown artists, born in the region. Many of the artists were trained in the best salons of Europe, while others were entirely self-taught. And while some visited for a single summer, others moved to Cape Ann and stayed for the remainder of their lives. The hope is that a broad and diverse survey has been attained, both known and unknown, those whose work has saturated art books and others whose most basic biographical data is still unknown.

A majority of the pictures in this book came from private collections, and have been reproduced here for the first time. Many gems from 'minor' artists were discovered in this way, which will hopefully foster renewed interest in their careers.

Much thought was given to how the artists would be sequenced. Although artists of certain styles, Impressionism or Modernists, did arrive in "waves," there were so many painters of various techniques working simultaneously on Cape Ann that to arrange them purely by their techniques would imply an artificial continuity from era to era. It was decided to arrange the artists in order of when they arrived on Cape Ann. In only a few cases was this date impossible to determine. For those artists, their placement was based upon an educated guess.

I have always had an affinity for concise biographies about artists, illustrating general impressions or salient moments in their lives. Rather than placing an emphasis on analysis of a style or the "purpose" of a painting, I sought to give an impression of the lives of the painters themselves, their struggles, their training and their travels. This will hopefully enhance the reader's appreciation of how Cape Ann impacted an artist's career. By making reference to the experiences of painters abroad, I related Cape Ann to the larger art world during each era and alluded to the many European influences that expatriate painters brought back with them.

In the early stages of developing the book, the primary basis for artists' selections was how the artist contributed to or effected Cape Ann art. Yet, as the book continued to evolve, it became evident that the outstanding characteristic of an artist's experience was how, instead, Cape Ann had effected the art of the painter. The unique quality of sunlight, the color and texture of the landscape, and even the mere quality and freshness of the air, have often brought about dramatic changes to painters' techniques and subject matter. In many cases these changes became a pivotal moment in the artists' development.

It is my hope that this book will increase awareness and appreciation of the rich history and prestige of Cape Ann—a region steeped in creative labor, whose own modesty and classic provincial indifference to self-promotion may have sometimes deprived it of its full recognition within the wider circles of American art.

FOR ALMOST two centuries, artists have been coming to Cape Ann, drawing a diverse roster of salon painters, Folk artists, Luminists, Tonalists, Impressionists, Ashcan painters, magazine and children's book illustrators, and Modernists alike. Somehow, each successive wave of artists found something on Cape Ann that they recognized as uniquely their own—uniquely for them.

Cape Ann's legacy of artists is astonishing—a veritable who's who of American art: Fitz Hugh Lane, William Morris Hunt, Winslow Homer, Childe Hassam, John H. Twachtman, John Sloan, Edward Hopper, Stuart Davis and Marsden Hartley all visited and painted on Cape Ann. Yet as the list grew, Cape Ann never lost its popularity as a place for both amateur and professional painters. Rejecting exclusivity, it is this egalitarian quality, characteristic of a rustic, working-class tradition that has renewed Cape Ann again and again, never growing tired of its painters while its painters never grew tired of it.

Long before the arrival of painters, however, Cape Ann was known for its industries. Established in 1623, Gloucester eventually became a prosperous port city in overseas trade. Later, as a deep water harbor, it provided close access to the North Atlantic fishing waters, establishing Gloucester as a major center for fishing. Sail making was also an important industry on the Cape, and Essex became a major center for shipbuilding. By the beginning of the nineteenth century, Rockport, originally known as Sandy Bay, became a prime location for quarrying stone, supplying granite for buildings, and paving blocks for streets in Boston and other cities along the east coast. These industries brought waves of immigrants looking for work. From Canada, Ireland, Portugal, Sicily, and Italy, men poured into Gloucester to work on the ships, establishing their own quarters in the city, bringing with them their traditions. In Rockport, Scandinavian men, especially Finns and Swedes, brought their families and labored in the rock quarries, establishing communities around Folly Cove and Pigeon Cove. Commerce from as far away as Dutch Surinam brought a variety of foreign goods to Gloucester, producing a bustling harbor city with a wondrous variety of languages, faces, and cultures.

It was the very image of Gloucester Harbor and the awesome spectacle of fleets of vessels with full open sails, that built Gloucester's reputation as indescribably picturesque. As the number of visiting artists increased, local fishermen weren't always sure what to make of them, showing up with canvas and paints, getting excited over light qualities and the way the color of the boats reflected upon the water. A little uncertain of their intentions, perhaps a little reluctant to accept the contrasts of their two professions, a quote from a turn of the century fisherman captures the feeling:

"What is it sickens with disgust the Gloucester sailorman?
Its these everlastin' artists a'setting all around.
A 'paintin' everything we do from the top mast to the ground...
For they puts us into picters and they think its just immense.
They call it 'picturesque,' b'lieve, but it certain isn't sense." 1

However, without established, reputable art schools in any of the major cities, the development of art in the region, as in the rest of America, was a slow process. Some of the earliest professional painters in the Cape Ann area came because local merchants, wealthy from international trade, wished to have their portraits painted. American painter John Singleton Copley completed several portraits of Gloucester merchants in the late eighteenth century. However it was a local young man from Gloucester in the mid-nineteenth century named Fitz Hugh Lane who would first put Cape Ann on the map.

With the increased popularity of Lane's works throughout New England in the 1850's, a stream of artists began to migrate to the region. Over 150 years later, that stream has never stopped and has at times overflowed. It was the man-made industries of Gloucester Harbor that first attracted artists, however, it was not long before the natural landscape also became an attraction. The inlets of Annisquam, the intimate streets of Lanesville, and the strange allure of Dogtown would draw painters back again and again. The birth of industrial power saw the disappearance of the majestic sailing fleets in Gloucester, but their replacement with engine-powered fishing boats of diverse colors had changed one muse for another.

In the late nineteenth century, many American art students felt they had to go to Europe for a proper art education. This sometimes created what could be called the 'John Singer Sargent syndrome'; for an American in Europe, bombarded by beautiful architecture, esteemed salons and centuries of rich art history, the temptation to stay in what was accepted as the center of the art world, was quite strong. Of the

65 artists featured in this book, roughly 42 studied and lived in Europe. Yet they all decided to return home, trading experiences in St. Ives, Brittany or Giverny for what they found in Cape Ann.

Some painters came seeking out the commotion of Gloucester Harbor, others for the serenity of the land. Cape Ann has been a surprising draw for painters from New York, Philadelphia, Cincinnati, the Midwest, and from the salons of Europe. While art on Cape Ann originally depicted local industries, and then its natural beauty, tourism eventually became another catalyst for growth in the area in the late nineteenth century. Sales of Cape Ann subject matter in other regions of America spread the popularity to a wider audience. Tourists visiting Cape Ann in the summer months bought paintings from artists in the local galleries; this provided a living for artists which, in turn, attracted more artists. This cycle continued throughout the twentieth century and in many ways guaranteed the continuation of the colony.

Artists had been coming to the Cape for more than sixty years before the first local art associations were founded. The Gallery-on-the-Moors, established in 1916, was a short lived exhibition space in Gloucester founded by William and Emmeline Atwood. The Gallery-on-the-Moors was the first public exhibition space of its kind to give local painters a chance to show their work. Later in 1921, the Rockport Art Association was formed, and the following year, the Gloucester Art Association was established, later changing its name to the North Shore Arts Association. Both remain active today.

Perhaps the best symbol of the legacy created by the migration of artists can be found in the form of a small red lobstermens' shack located at the end of a wharf on Bearskin Neck in Rockport. Built around the time of the Civil War, its prominent position at the end of the pier made it a natural backdrop for artists painting harbor pictures. Finally in the early 1930's, while critiquing a group of students' pictures, several of which featured the little red shack, Lester Hornby, using a term often employed by French students to describe frequently painted sites, exclaimed, "What— Motif No. 1 again!" His fateful words stuck and since then the little red shack has been referred to as "Motif No. 1." It is thought to be the most frequently painted building in the United States.

Cape Ann's continued appeal for artists is confirmed by the sheer quantity of thousands of painters who have painted along the shores. The area has also never succumbed to the influence of a single dominant painter-teacher. Unlike John Carlson in Woodstock or Charles Hawthorne among Provincetown

The Red Sail Boat   CA. 1930 OIL ON CANVAS 32" X 26"
H. BOYLSTON DUMMER   PRIVATE COLLECTION
PHOTO COURTESY OF DAVIES FINE ARTS

painters, no single Cape Ann artist, through the popularity of his pictures or the influence of his teaching, has ever been so dominant as to define a single "look" for Cape Ann. This has ensured a variety of work among generations of painters and freed Cape Ann from the limits such a definition would instill.

Many of the changes and trends in American art can be traced through a survey of work produced on Cape Ann over the decades. While the area has been known for representational art and a conservative attitude towards progressive styles, the twentieth century in fact saw the arrival of artists to Cape Ann of almost every conceivable style and approach. Beautiful harbors and sailing vessels attracted realist painters in a time when the academic tradition was king. Cape Ann soon became a haven for many of the painters experimenting with Impressionism. With its emphasis on light and color, the play of sunlight on water alone was enough to draw painters back year after year. Because of its geography, the light on Cape Ann offered a great array of contrasts. Clear sunlight, dense fog, horrific storms, brilliant sunsets and hazy dawns with milky light seem to follow each other in rapid succession. Later, the Ashcan painters were drawn to the activity and the increasingly industrialized elements of the harbors.

Cape Ann's popularity with artists did not wain or die with the popularity of one particular style, or evolution of art. If it had, the appeal of Cape Ann would have revealed its own limitations. Instead, Cape Ann continues to redefine itself as painters redefine their art.

*pages 97, 99, 103, 134,

FITZ HUGH LANE

1804 - 1865

CAPE ANN HAD painters before Fitz Hugh Lane who produced images of the region, but Lane was truly Cape Ann's first native artist. Working from a relatively remote environment he was an early Luminist painter and a major contributor to popularizing the style among other mid-century artists. In many ways he legitimized Gloucester in a national cultural context, bringing it wide acclaim with exhibitions of his work. His images gave the region a new identity, establishing the foundation of a great legacy for the colony that has survived and transcended every change in the art world.

Lane was a native of Gloucester, born at a time when the town was a bustling harbor prospering from foreign trade. His roots in the region go back to 1707 when his great-great grandfather came to Cape Ann and with other members of the extended Lane family established Lanesville.

When only eighteen months old, Lane showed symptoms of a disease, most likely polio, which left him crippled. Though he did grow to full height, for the rest of his life he walked with crutches. Given the name Nathaniel Rogers Lane at birth, he changed it while a young man.

Deprived of the natural vigor for outdoor play possessed by other young boys, Lane took to drawing and sketching. With the absence of any permanent artists-in-residence, he taught himself the skills. In the early 1830's Lane worked for a print shop in Gloucester called "Clegg and Dodge." Perhaps it was this environment which first exposed him to opportunities elsewhere, for in 1832 Lane decided to move to Boston where he began an apprenticeship with the lithographer William S. Pendleton. Under Pendleton he received his first formal artistic training, at twenty eight years old.

Calm Seas
1847 OIL ON CANVAS 9 1/2" X 13 1/2"
PRIVATE COLLECTION
PHOTO COURTESY OF GODEL & CO., FINE ART

(OPPOSITE)

Gloucester Harbor at Sunrise
CA. 1850 OIL ON CANVAS 24" X 36"
COLLECTION OF CAPE ANN HISTORICAL ASSOCIATION

Exposed to professional art and artists like the British marine painter Robert Salmon, Boston was a crucial, formative period for Lane. He worked intensely in a variety of mediums, making periodic sketching trips back to Cape Ann. In 1836 he made his first lithographs of Gloucester harbor entitled *View of the Town of Gloucester, Mass.* In 1845, Lane began his own firm in Boston called "Lane and Scott's Lithography, Boston." In 1846 he produced another view of Gloucester harbor which became very popular and sold a large number of prints. The profits Lane made enabled him to make perhaps the most crucial decision of his life, to return at age 42 to the city of his birth, rather than remaining in Boston closer to galleries and commission work.

In 1847 Fitz Hugh Lane returned to Gloucester, then undergoing an economic boom in the fishing industry. Having left the town as a self-taught artist, he returned a trained draftsman with commercial experience, business savvy and greater financial freedom. In 1849 he designed a stone house on a hillside behind Duncan's Point in the Harbor Village. Still a monument and an icon of the town today, Lane lived and worked in the sturdy, granite house for the remainder of his life. Many of his best known paintings were created from the third floor panoramic view overlooking the harbor.

Lane's early works in Boston hinted at his future potential. Created in a commercial capacity, they also function as a historical record and a topographical survey of the port. In this respect, Lane served not merely as an artist but as an historian and a surveyor; as Elizabeth Ellis describes, "He became the taxonomer of the Gloucester Coast." 2

One can trace the development of Lane's style through the evolution of his portrayal of harbors and the sea. Lane's earlier work is more anecdotal, with great activity, emphasizing movement and the action of ships and men. Like ship portraiture in the Anglo-Dutch tradition, they seem to capture a moment in time. As direct and reflected light became more important to Lane, evolving to the style that would later be called Luminism, he grew more concerned with conveying a feeling rather than a view. His paintings became less populated with ships or people; activity and movement decreased dramatically, creating a great sense of stillness. By the 1850's until his death in 1865, Lane's work lost the scientific, formal quality often associated with earlier American marine art, passing from the anecdotal to the eternal. No longer the "taxonomer of Gloucester," Lane became its poet.

Both painted in 1847, *The Fort and Ten Pound Island* and *Calm Seas* are prime examples of Lane's work as it evolved. Many historians point to the early 1850's as the beginning of Lane's Luminist period. These two pictures show that Lane was experimenting with the transparent and reflective light of Luminism before then. With the foreground activity and the variety of boats in the water *The Fort and Ten Pound Island* has elements of Lane's earlier narrative quality. But *Calm Seas* has been reduced to its simplest elements. Far less busy than his earlier harbor pictures, it is serenity not activity that prevails. With a variety of whites and greys, Lane achieves a sort of silver luminism in the picture. The distant ship is obscured by mist. Distance and light have become hypnotic. Unlike early ship portraiture,

View of the Town of Gloucester
1836 LITHOGRAPH 15" X 21 1/2"
PRIVATE COLLECTION

(PAGES 10 - 11)

The Fort and Ten Pound Island
1847 OIL ON CANVAS 20" X 30"
PRIVATE COLLECTION
PHOTO COURTESY OF
HIRSCHL & ADLER GALLERIES, INC.

Western Shore with Norman's Woe
1862 OIL ON CANVAS 21" X 35 1/2"
COLLECTION OF CAPE ANN HISTORICAL ASSOCIATION

the specific identity of the vessel in *Calm Seas* is no longer a major element in the picture.

Lane's progress from academic and narrative to luminist and poetic was neither linear nor rapid. Never having the opportunity to travel or study in Europe, Lane's evolution was largely a self-generated one. Unlike many later American painters whose exposure to French masters seemed to change their style overnight, Lane's progression from "taxonomer" to Luminist was achieved not in the salons of an influential master, but alone at his easel before a harbor.

Fitz Hugh Lane was a popular figure in town. Local newspapers advertised shows of his new work. Though Lane's physical disabilities certainly limited his travel, he did make several trips throughout the 1850's around New England, often to Maine, and he may have once visited Puerto Rico. His popularity spread, thus drawing other marine painters to Cape Ann, a trend that has continued for a hundred and fifty years.

Lane never married. How the psychological trauma of his disabilities affected his painting or his decision not to marry is uncertain. His decision to remain permanently in Gloucester however would forever ally the name of his birthplace with the cannon of great nineteenth century artists. While other nineteenth century painters like Bierstadt, Church, Kensett, Gifford and Cropsey found fame precisely on their ability to travel great distances across the continent to paint its beauty, Lane did so with only a small range of views around the New England coast. Consequently, the Hudson River painters are not associated with anywhere in particular, but everywhere. Only Lane resides among the nineteenth century greats, having lived in a small town. Confined to his crutches and living without the companionship of a wife, Lane captured the serenity and wonders of nature, which he may have recognized as his greatest and only consolation for a difficult life.

Evening in Gloucester Harbor
1871 OIL ON CANVAS 20" X 40"
PRIVATE OWNER
PHOTO COURTESY OF BROWN CORBIN FINE ART

FRANCIS AUGUSTUS SILVA

1835 - 1886

ONE OF THE MOST poetic Luminist painters of the nineteenth century, Silva enfused drama and mood into his pictures that some critics of the time described as Transcendentalist. Though Silva drew from a very early age, he did not pursue art professionally until he was discharged from the Union army after service in the Civil War. Born in New York City, Silva developed an early fascination with coastal settings and was most likely familiar with various New England shore communities before he painted them. After the Civil War Silva set up residence in New York, exhibiting a coastal scene in 1868 at the National Academy of Design.

He then began to travel the shores of the Eastern seaboard, painting the Chesapeake Bay, Coney Island, Rockaway and the North Shore of Massachusetts. In fact, Silva's earliest surviving painting is simply entitled *Cape Ann*, dated 1870. One of Silva's better documented trips to the North Shore came in the late summer of 1871 when he visited Annisquam, Thacher Island and Bass Rocks.

Evening in Gloucester Harbor is a stunning example of Silva's unique sensibility for light, hue and glow. His pictures bear elements of the fantastic, characteristic of the Hudson River School; but they also have a remarkable quality of light and color similar to the work of the Orientalists. Luminist painters were determined to convey more than the mere appearance of a place. The writings of Emerson and Transcendentalism influenced many artists to strive to capture the spiritual essence of nature. *Evening in Gloucester Harbor* is a very early example of Silva capturing these tenets of Luminism. Though the influence of Fitz Hugh Lane is apparent, Silva's picture bears closer resemblance to the golden luminism of Sanford Gifford than to Lane's silver luminism.

Bathed in orange and red, Gloucester takes on the appearance of an exotic foreign port. Because of the intensity of warm light, even the white sails are transformed into a shade of orange, reminding one of paintings of Venice, a city Silva would later visit and paint. This may be the litmus of a great painter, perhaps what is most original about nineteenth century Luminist paintings: to see what is commonplace in an entirely new way, as though seeing it for the first time. Silva perceives Gloucester the way an American might see the Bosphorus in Constantinople or Aberdeen Harbor in Hong Kong. He views it with the eyes of a foreigner. The sublime qualities of sea, sky and sails are emphasized by the euphoric blending of reflection and the transparency of light which were the basis of the Luminist approach. *Evening in Gloucester Harbor* is consistent with the work Silva would produce over the next several years. Perfecting an approach, Silva experimented with moonlight and other natural effects but resisted the Impressionistic concepts that were beginning to influence American artists.

Silva once wrote that he was sure Impressionism would eventually be "consigned to the rubbish heap." [3] With his death from pneumonia in 1886, he did not live to see Impressionism rejuvenate the colony and spark a whole new era in Cape Ann art.

Sea Smoke
CA. 1890 OIL ON CANVAS 30" X 50"
COLLECTION OF STORY PARSONS

GILBERT TUCKER MARGESON

1852 – 1949

IF FITZ HUGH LANE is Gloucester's original native son, then surely Tucker Margeson occupies that place as Rockport artists' founding father. He opened up the first artist studio in Rockport in 1873 when he was only twenty one. Known as the Dean of the Rockport Colony, Margeson was born in Nova Scotia and came to the United States when he was nine years old. His roots in the New World trace back to the Mayflower, where an ancestor of his signed the original Compact.

With early instruction under Alfred Ordway, Margeson maintained his interest in art while working a variety of jobs. When Margeson came to Cape Ann in 1870, his first action in fact was to find a job at the Western Union Office in Gloucester. Later he opened the Margeson stationery store in Rockport, a variety store that had the town's first modest array of art supplies. For years Margeson maintained his store, also working later as the town tax collector, but always working at his marine pictures, bold and dramatic images of ships in crashing surf, struggling against waves and froth. His pictures became quite popular with locals and found their way on the walls of businesses and local banks, where many can still be found today.

From his Atlantic Avenue studio, overlooking the harbor, Margeson watched Rockport slowly transform itself, from a town of few artists and many fishermen, when paintings were a novelty, to an art colony with a long legacy that has seen the presence of many of America's greatest painters. One of his marine pictures hangs in the Naval Office in Washington D.C. In 1921, when the formation of the Rockport Art Association announced the formal birth of the art colony, Margeson, its oldest member, was already 70 years old.

WINSLOW HOMER

1836 – 1910

WHEN WINSLOW HOMER made his first extended visit to Cape Ann in 1873, he was known only as an illustrator for popular magazines. Though already 37 years old, he was not yet a respected painter; he had not yet changed the course of American art. However, Homer had distinguished himself during the Civil War with illustrations for *Harper's Weekly*. After the war, he concerned himself with the changing nature of America, the transition of the veteran from soldier to family man and the recollection of simpler times, often depicted through the imagery of boyhood. Already a witness to a changing America, Homer's stay on Cape Ann solidified a theme of "tracking" the evolution of Americanness, which changed as his art changed.

Some pictures from 1869 and 1871 suggest Homer may have previously visited Gloucester, but his first documented trip came in June of 1873. Residing in the Atlantic House over the summer, Homer completed several images of boats, docks and locals, but the most significant developments were Homer's singular use of watercolor and his depiction of local Gloucester boys. Watercolor had always been associated with Sunday painters and as a medium for sketching. Watercolor images received little respect in most American exhibitions. Though used as the basis for his illustrations, Homer also intended them as finished pictures, thus to some degree risking the integrity of his name and reputation.

Continuing his preoccupation with youth and boyhood, Homer produced several pictures of young boys playing, sailing and day dreaming. However, there was a dramatic change in the nature of the images. In contrast to Homer's Twain-esque *Snap the Whip*, painted just the previous year, a nostalgic icon of American boyhood,

Breezing Up (A Fair Wind)
1873–1876 OIL ON CANVAS 24" X 38"
GIFT OF THE W.L. AND MAY T. MELLON FOUNDATION
COPYRIGHT 2000 BOARD OF TRUSTEES,
NATIONAL GALLERY OF ART, WASHINGTON, D.C.

(OPPOSITE)

Sailing Out of Gloucester
1880 WATERCOLOR ON PAPER 13" X 19"
COURTESY OF CANAJOHARIE LIBRARY
AND ART GALLERY

See Saw
1873 WATERCOLOR ON PAPER 7" X 13"
COURTESY OF CANAJOHARIE LIBRARY
AND ART GALLERY

many of his Gloucester pictures depict boys, solitary in thought or place, staring distantly out to sea.

All fishing communities had their orphans and widows; such was the reality of livelihoods earned on the sea. In 1873 alone, 174 men from the region were lost at sea. In late August of the same year, a single storm sunk nine boats, killing 128 fishermen. Such disasters left young boys on the shore, searching for their fathers on the horizon. Homer most likely observed such boys, and the change in his perception of youth is undeniable. In many images, Homer very often hides their faces, obscuring them behind hats or turning them away to face the ocean. Such techniques deprive the viewer of a readable expression, suggesting the facelessness of orphans whose future is in the balance. Many of these young boys would grow up to be fishermen, raising children who would come to fear for their safety. Such notions are quite readable in Homer's Cape Ann pictures. Homer's groundbreaking experiments with watercolor and this emotional, yet unsentimental quality make a single summer's stay in Gloucester a watershed in American art.

In the seven years that separate Homer's two stays in Gloucester, there were many significant changes. In 1875, Homer stopped his illustration work. Concentrating on his own art, he repeat-

edly reused sketches from his first stay to create additional Gloucester subjects. Working from memory and from previously painted watercolors, Homer produced some of his best Gloucester work while not in Gloucester, like the famous *Breezing Up*, painted in 1875.

Despite some positive praise, Homer received much criticism for his loose, unfinished looking pictures at New York exhibitions in the late 1870's. He was not unaffected by such criticism. Upon returning to Gloucester in the summer of 1880, he sought the isolation of living in a lighthouse on Ten Pound Island, venturing inland only for supplies. Though sometimes socializing with a few local fishermen, some writers mark this as the beginning of Homer's reclusive tendencies.

Homer's Gloucester images from his second visit reflect his change in residences. People are still present but are often less obvious in much of his work from 1880. The Gloucester boys, rather than the focus of the image, psychologically separated from the landscape, now blend with their surroundings. From Ten Pound Island, Homer had a perfect view of departing and arriving ships. Schooners and boats become more prevalent under a variety of weather and light conditions. Many of Homer's images are also incredibly loose by the standards of the day. The completed composition, characteristic of an illus-

The Lobster Pot
1880 WATERCOLOR ON PAPER 9 1/2" X 13 1/4"
PRIVATE COLLECTION
PHOTO COURTESY OF SOTHEBY'S

trator, was replaced by impressions and use of negative space. Through his mastery of the watercolor technique in the intervening years, he attained a variety of light and atmospheric effects, covering less of the paper with paint, using the white of the paper to produce dazzling light effects.

Before Cape Ann, Homer had shown hints of interest in the sea, but his stays in Gloucester fostered a life-long fascination with the sea that car-ried him from Tynemouth, England to Prouts Neck to the Caribbean twenty years later. Homer's time on Cape Ann had been brief. His first time as an illustrator, his second visit already as a slightly hermitic painter, he did not draw other artists to the region. He did not open a school or create a colony of followers. He did, however, contribute mightily to defining the legacy of Gloucester, and equally, Gloucester forever changed the art of Winslow Homer.

WILLIAM MORRIS HUNT

1824 - 1879

AN INTRIGUING, AND tragic figure, William Morris Hunt was a major force in American art, particularly in Boston. Hunt abandoned his studies at Harvard and began studying in Paris with the renowned painter Thomas Couture in 1847. Exposure to Couture and later to Jean-François Millet thoroughly convinced Hunt of the genius of French art. Returning to Boston in 1855 a passionate advocate of the French Barbizon style, Hunt encouraged Boston families to collect the work years before the style had become popular in America.

Hunt became a profoundly influential teacher, encouraging a spontaneity in sketching and brushwork, stressing the importance of capturing a feeling over a perfect rendering of an image that long preceded the Impressionistic influence in America. Finding success as a high society portrait painter, Hunt opened a school for women artists in the early 1870's that would become the source of some of the most talented young women painters of the era. It also became the backbone for the art colony that began around him in Magnolia.

The good fortune of Hunt's juggernaut career did not remain with him. In 1872, fire consumed his Summer Street studio in Boston, destroying an enormous body of his life's work and his collection of French art. This and other circumstances exacerbated a difficult marriage, and by 1875 his wife and children were no longer living with him. It was under the weight of this turbulence that Hunt came to Cape Ann in 1877.

Hunt's first time in the region came in 1859 when he had painted a portrait of a judge in Essex. Other painters had been to Magnolia before him, but Hunt's reputation and following brought a new recognition to the region. Arriving in June of 1877, Hunt purchased a local barn which was converted into a large studio, nicknamed "The Hulk" due to its resemblance to a stranded ship. With Helen Knowlton as his apprentice, the two spent the summer painting.

Suffering severe financial, artistic and emotional losses, Hunt nevertheless persevered and did not surrender his life nor abandon his art. Magnolia was the first place that Hunt began to explore landscape painting with a single-minded focus. Far from the city and the seekers of portraits, the outdoors became Hunt's new obsession. Setting out each day in an enclosed carriage with his driver and assistant, Hunt would tour the countryside until he found an interesting view. Then his assistant would set up his easel and paints and he would begin his day's work. Some enduring images were produced that summer, including *Gloucester Harbor*; upon completion, Hunt is alleged to have said to Knowlton that he had "painted a picture with light in it."[4]

With Hunt establishing a new art colony, drawing students from Boston, it is difficult to imagine he would be dead in less than two years. He returned for six weeks the following summer before departing to work on a series of commissioned murals for the state capitol in Albany in 1878. The murals however were ruined shortly after completion due to water leaks in a faulty roof. Some say this was the final straw in a series of torments that Hunt could no longer bear. Aged and greyed beyond his 55 years, Hunt was found drowned in a pond on the Isle of Shoals in New Hampshire. Whether it was a dizzy spell or a deliberate act is still greatly disputed. But even before his death, Hunt's brief stay on Cape Ann had attracted other followers to the area, including Ellen Day Hale. The colony continued around "The Hulk" throughout the 1880's surrounding Helen Knowlton who recalled for others tales of the long bearded Mr. Hunt who spent two seasons of his short life on Cape Ann.

Gloucester Harbor

STEPHEN PARRISH

1846 – 1938

AT FIRST GLANCE, in the history of art, Stephen Parrish is most famous for being the father of one of the most celebrated American artists, Maxfield Parrish. A closer look, however, reveals that he was much more than just the father of greatness; after all he was the source of whatever gifts he instilled in his young son. However the pursuit of art was not a natural direction for Stephen Parrish who came from a legacy of lawyers, doctors and businessmen. Raised in a Quaker household, he was forced to hide in the attic of his home and draw clandestinely, for his parents thought art was sinful.

After some years spent in the coal and later the stationery business, Parrish's inner aspirations to pursue art finally made him break away from family tradition. Though Parrish would eventually concentrate on oil painting, his first intensive pursuit was in etching. His first lessons in the medium were from Peter Moran in Philadelphia in 1879, and the following year he took his first trip to Cape Ann. For some time he and his wife and young son Maxfield stayed at the Fairview Inn in East Gloucester but later established a studio in Annisquam. Over these years Parrish produced a number of excellent, very original etchings which sold well. Etchings were very popular in the 1880's and along with J.A.M. Whistler and Charles A. Platt, Parrish became one of the most popular etchers in the country. He was excited by all the coastal areas of New England, even working as far north as Nova Scotia. However he always returned to working in Annisquam and produced roughly 42 etchings of Cape Ann over the years. It is believed that *Gloucester Wharves* is among the largest, most ambitious of his Cape Ann etchings. Parrish would usually take long day trips, studying the landscape, often taking with him his wife and young Maxfield, nourishing his son's artistic aspirations.

With the decline of the commercial boom of etching, Parrish reverted to oil painting which he had neglected for many years. Later in his life he moved to Cornish, New Hampshire. While other artists spent more time in the region, Parrish's contribution to the art colony is significant for the simple fact that etchings existed in multiple images, making works available for a fraction of the price of an oil painting. Consequently Parrish's pictures of Cape Ann spread the region's fame and adorned the walls of homes and businesses that might have otherwise been left bare.

Gloucester (after W.M. Hunt)
1880 ETCHING 14" X 21"
COLLECTION OF THE CAPE ANN HISTORICAL ASSOCIATION

(OPPOSITE)
Gloucester Wharves
1880 ETCHING 21" X 14"
PRIVATE COLLECTION
PHOTO COURTESY OF DAVIES FINE ARTS

WILLIAM LAMB PICKNELL

1853 – 1897

PICKNELL'S FIRST exposure to art most likely occurred in Boston where he befriended George Inness Jr., son of the great landscape painter. With the loss of his father at an early age, Picknell and his mother moved from his native Vermont to join relatives in Boston. By the time he was a young man, Picknell convinced his relatives to lend him the tidy sum of $1,000 to study in Europe. He left for Italy with George Inness Jr. and stayed in the Inness household, studying with George Inness. Later, Picknell settled in France where he trained under the renowned master Jean-Léon Gérôme. Eventually Picknell settled in Pont-Aven where he found the generosity of inn keepers and friends sustained him long after his funds had vanished.

Often painting in the company of Hugh Bolton Jones and Robert Wylie, Picknell's years of living on borrowed time and money paid off with the acclaim he won for his now famous painting *The Road to Concarneau*. This significantly changed his stature in art circles and freed him to travel and paint in Britain. For the next two years the popularity of his pictures increased and Picknell found himself more and more renowned among European collectors. In 1881, he returned to Boston, as legend goes, with not a single picture in his possession; they had all sold. Shortly after returning he made his first trip to Cape Ann. Looking at Picknell's work from his European years, one is struck by the fact that his pictures don't look like those of an expatriate, an

Man in a Boat
CA. 1883 - 1891 OIL ON CANVAS 29 1/2" X 39 1/2"
PHOTO COURTESY OF THE WILLIAM LAMB PICKNELL CATALOGUE RAISONNE PROJECT

Wingaersheek Creek Beach, Gloucester
CA. 1887 OIL ON CANVAS 48" X 79"
PHOTO COURTESY OF ADELSON GALLERIES, INC.

(PAGES 26 - 27)
Clam Diggers
1888 OIL ON CANVAS 29 3/4" X 43 3/4"
PHOTO COURTESY OF THE WILLIAM LAMB PICKNELL
CATALOGUE RAISONNE PROJECT

American with European training; they look like the work of a European. The palette is dark, more moody. In all respects, Picknell came to Cape Ann as a European painter.

It is fascinating that Picknell did not explore figure painting to any significant degree while in Europe. He stuck largely to landscape scenes. This is what makes his Cape Ann work all the more refreshing. Nothing like *Man in a Boat* is known to exist in his European body of work. Painted most likely in one of the Annisquam inlets, Picknell's period studying under teachers like Gérôme, a master figure painter, now reveals itself. As his work is described by many critics, this picture is both realist and naturalist in approach. It is rustic and hearty but not senti-mentalized. It is neither romantic nor is it of the social realist approach so popular in France at the

time. It is for all intents and purposes, natural. The fisherman is strong and vibrant. One can see the tension on the oars in his tightened forearms. The color is muted under an overcast sky. It gives the picture a European quality reminiscent of the great British marine painter Stanhope Forbes, who was painting during the same period.

The Road to Concarneau was being exhibited with great enthusiasm in Boston while Picknell was working in nearby Annisquam. Picknell's pres-ence there also attracted several of his artist friends from the British and French colonies who were visiting America. Picknell married in 1889 and the two returned to Europe. Deteriorating health brought about by the loss of his child and a five year struggle with malaria hastened his death, which occurred in 1897 shortly after returning to America. He was 43.

PARKER PERKINS

1862 - 1942

PARKER PERKINS MAY perhaps be the embodiment of what is most fundamental about Cape Ann artists. As a marine painter he was never widely known or celebrated outside of the region and his reputation as an artist was eclipsed by many of the later painters that arrived on Cape Ann, formally trained in New York, Boston or Europe. One hundred years later, his name is among the more obscure group that made up the very early years of the art colony. Yet his dedication and love of the region and the recollections of those who knew him seem the epitome of what is most peculiar and endearing about a painter.

After Tucker Margeson, Perkins was one of the first artists to settle in Rockport. Entirely a self-taught painter, Perkins left his hometown of Gardner, Massachusetts, married and arrived in Rockport, moving into a house on High Street. Thus began Perkin's relationship with the small coastal town where he became a local legend. Always dressed impeccably, often in a white suit in the summer, cane in hand, he would stroll about the town on his errands, greeting all those he met. His home was filled with as many as twenty cats that had free reign over the Perkins' household. He loved the ocean and found years of joy in painting marine pictures, many of which can still be found in homes around Rockport. Never regarding art, especially his own, as high brow or pretentious, he often gave away his paintings as gifts of friendship, tokens of gratitude or as payment for meals or other services.

Parker Perkins befriended many of the younger painters coming to town, helping them settle and acclimate. Eric Hudson met Perkins shortly after arriving in Rockport, and through him was introduced to Harrison Cady. Perkins also taught classes to locals and summer visitors who desired a lesson. He would often advise his students with such words as, "Good gad, satisfaction's all there is to it. You paint the dollar sign and you're done for."[5] Perhaps his most significant act as a teacher came when he met a young local boy with great artistic potential, by the name of William Lester Stevens, and gave him his first art lessons. Anecdotes of Perkin's life do not detract from the fact that he loved painting, loved the water and was ultimately most at home by the shore in front of his easel. The Boston Herald critic Lawrence Dame best captured the essence of Parker Perkins, and perhaps of any artist:

"Whenever the artist cannot be seen, bright and dapper, bowing his way through the streets of Rockport, he may be found, if it is a stormy day, braced like some ancient deity on the cliffs along the turbulent shore....A little man, rich in soul, who has the magical power of keeping the seas alive on canvas, a happy philosopher, finding his greatest joy of living in his work." [6]

(OPPOSITE)
Two Schooners
1892 OIL ON CANVAS 36" X 26"
COLLECTION OF ROCKPORT NATIONAL BANK

AUGUSTUS W. BUHLER

1853 – 1920

AUGUSTUS BUHLER spent most of his career among the fishermen of Gloucester, striving to capture the reality of a life so often romanticized by artists. Born in New York City, Buhler had first learned the methods of an artist from his father who worked doing gold striping on horse carriages. After the family moved to Worcester, Massachusetts, Buhler began studies at the Boston Art Club. He and his wife moved to Annisquam in 1885, living for three years in a converted fishermen's shack. Here he developed a compassion and respect for the lives of individual fishermen, their stories and their daily toil.

In 1888, Buhler went to Paris for two years and studied at the Académie Julian. Buhler found most Barbizon artists, fond of painting farming life, simply didn't understand its hardships. He believed a closer understanding and trust between painter and subject was vital for the integrity of the picture, out of respect for the person represented.

Returning to Massachusetts in 1890, Buhler established homes in Boston and Annisquam. While teaching and illustrating for *Harper's Weekly*, he set about to attain his goal: the faithful, truthful representation of the men who make their living at sea. By befriending the fishermen he sought to reduce the distance and skepticism many of them held towards painters. He painted them in the extreme contrasts of their job, from the labor of navigating a storm to the lazy hours in a harbor shack.

Eventually Buhler moved to East Gloucester, teaching on Rocky Neck and painting the beloved "walrus-mustached"[7] old fishermen up close, inviting them to sit in his studio. Often the younger fishermen would join them, gathering around his studio, eager for a peek at the picture or a jab at their skippers. In time Buhler earned the respect of the local men and in return saw their unguarded candor, humor and toughness.

Buhler's 'heroic marine' illustrations helped to create the respect among a larger audience for these men of the sea. Buhler always believed that an artist could, or even should, be an historian, capturing an era that was changing, fleeting or disappearing. Buhler had a particular fondness for painting older fishermen with their bearded, worn and hearty faces, for he knew,

"Few men who fish on the Bank live to be old—the result is there are comparatively few old fishermen in Gloucester."[8]

GEORGE W. HARVEY
1855 - 1930

WITH THE EXCEPTION of Fitz Hugh Lane, perhaps no artist could be thought of more as a native of Cape Ann than George W. Harvey. Born in Gloucester, Harvey was the son of a sea captain and grew up looking at the paintings of Fitz Hugh Lane. An early interest in art led to some training with the artist W.H. Weisman, but Harvey is considered to have been largely a self-taught painter.

Marrying a local photographer, Martha Hale Rogers, the two took a long trip to Europe in 1884, spending a majority of their time in Holland. Outside of his own exposure to local Cape Ann art, it was the Dutch school of painters that had the strongest influence on Harvey. Indeed his pictures exhibit a Dutch, academic sensibility and bear little resemblance to the French Impressionistic style that influenced so many painters who have worked on Cape Ann. Harvey flourished in Holland and was made an honorary member of the Royal Dutch Society of Artists. He returned to Cape Ann in the late 1880's and painted extensively throughout the region. By 1900 he had set up a studio in Annisquam, working in watercolor and oils, and even began experimenting with etching as a medium.

Spearing Flounders is certainly Harvey's masterpiece. Though the image has the icon quality of a Winslow Homer, it is entirely original in perspective, approach and light treatment. Other Harvey pictures reveal a similar fascination with fog and mist and their use to create large vacant spaces in a composition. Nowhere did he master this phenomenon better than in *Spearing Flounders*. Harvey stripped the image to its fundamental elements, minimizing the ingredients so that the viewer feels he is seeing nothing extraneous. Harvey's sense of control and restraint is masterful. The temptation perhaps to paint additional objects has been quelled, leaving the viewer with the base elements: a dory, a patient fisherman, the green hue of a reflection and the magnificent silence of the water. The milky haze that obscures the distance is reminiscent of Luminism. The image is hypnotic; what is most often depicted as laborious and dangerous or romanticized and colorful becomes under Harvey's perception a Zen-like practice, emphasizing the deep meditation of the method, the tranquility of the surroundings and the calm of the fisherman who is entranced in an act that seems almost mystical. The viewer is left hearing only the slight sound of a wooden vessel slipping through still water.

Remarkably, *Spearing Flounders* is a largely unknown image and has never before been reproduced in color. Harvey is not an artist usually considered among the cannon of great Cape Ann painters. His work is known only to a relative few. Yet like the work of fellow Gloucester native Fitz Hugh Lane, there is a shimmer in Harvey's painting which suggests that growing up right in the region instilled in him an understanding of the pure essence of man and water.

Spearing Flounders
CA. 1890 OIL ON CANVAS 30" X 44"
PRIVATE COLLECTION
PHOTO COURTESY OF VOSE GALLERIES

Spearing Flounders, Salt Island Bar
ETCHING 3 3/4" X 5"
COLLECTION OF MR. AND MRS. WILLIAM TRAYES

ELLEN DAY HALE

1855 - 1940

ELLEN DAY HALE was born into one of the most prominent Boston families of the era; the daughter of the novelist Edward Everett Hale, her extended family included the orator Nathan Hale and Harriet Beecher Stowe, author of *Uncle Tom's Cabin*. Her younger brother, Philip Leslie Hale, was also an important artist. Although she became an acclaimed still-life and landscape painter, it was her elegant portraits and figural pieces that set Hale apart from so many other painters of the era, male or female. Her early studies were with Dr. William Rimmer in 1873. Following this, Hale joined a new atelier for women opened by William Morris Hunt. She was nineteen years old.

Hunt's importance and influence among art circles in Boston at the time cannot be overemphasized. His advocation of the French Barbizon style and the importance of artists studying abroad motivated her to make the trip with Hunt's assistant, Helen Knowlton, in 1881. While in Europe, her training included attendance at the Académie Colarossi and the Académie Julian. After returning to America, Hale exhibited at the Pennsylvania Academy and began a series of trips throughout the country. Beginning in the late 1880's Hale established a residence at Folly Cove in Rockport. By the mid 1890's she built an adjoining studio nicknamed

"The Thickets," due to the wild plums that grew around the property. For many summers throughout her career Hale returned there, usually in the company of friends and visitors, including Philip Leslie Hale, his wife Lilian Westcott Hale and Cecilia Beaux.

Hale was very impressed and influenced by the techniques of Hunt and the French Barbizon painters as well as the traditional Boston School "look," made popular by painters like William Paxton. More impressionistic than her earlier figure work, *Morning News* seems the very essence of elegance, a symbol of turn-of-the-century Victorian regality. Set against a dark backdrop, illuminated by a soft, glowing, Vermeer-like light source, *Morning News* is the quintessential Boston style. Painted in 1905, the rendering of the woman's profile, delicate but not frail, and the subtleties of light and color in her hair and hands reveal the growth and maturity of Hale's skills. With the beginning of a new industrial century, *Morning News* is nostalgic for a different era.

Hale's later work on Cape Ann focused increasingly on the surrounding landscape. She also began to experiment with etching. In her later years she was a frequent exhibitor at the North Shore Arts Association. A memorial exhibition of her work was held there in 1940 after her death.

(OPPOSITE)
Morning News
1905 OIL ON CANVAS 50" X 36"
PRIVATE COLLECTION

FRANK DUVENECK

1848 – 1919

DUVENECK IS now regarded as one of the most influential American painters of the late nineteenth century. Born in Kentucky, and later associated with Cincinnati, Duveneck first spent several years apprenticing for a career in church decoration. Eventually the urge to become an artist sent Duveneck to Munich where he studied at the Royal Academy of Art in 1870. He developed exceptional skills in "the Munich style" of painting and is perhaps the American artist who is most associated with the city. He spent the next twenty years crisscrossing the Atlantic, spending a majority of his time in Europe.

Duveneck's bohemian lifestyle was very similar to his contemporary, John Singer Sargent. He lived a life most can only dream of, traveling from one end of Europe to the other, painting and exhibiting, often in the company of William Merritt Chase and John H. Twachtman. He worked with great intensity, painting constantly and before long was teaching an increasing number of other young American painters known simply as the "Duveneck Boys." Rather than spending one or two token years of study in

Europe, Duveneck was becoming something of a permanent expatriate.

While in Munich in 1879, he met Elizabeth Boott, a painter from a Boston family who had seen his work and sought him out while in Europe. The two became involved and together made their first trip to Cape Ann in 1883. It is believed he did not produce any pictures during his first trip to Gloucester. The two returned to Europe and painted throughout Italy and later moved to Paris. In 1886 they were married and had a son. Several accounts of the two painting and traveling together reveal a kindred bond between the couple that made her death in 1888 from pneumonia all the more devastating for him.

Duveneck returned to America and spent the next several years constantly moving about. He returned to Cape Ann in 1890 where he taught a summer course with Theodore Wendel at Helen Knowlton's School. In 1892, he spent his first full summer in Gloucester, staying in the famous Harbor View Hotel. Later on he rented a home on Eastern Point. From then on, until 1917 he spent all of his summers on Cape Ann. Over the

Horizon at Gloucester
CA. 1900 OIL ON CANVAS 24" X 35"
PRIVATE COLLECTION

(OPPOSITE)
Yellow Shed From Banner Hill
1905 OIL ON CANVAS 36" X 40"
PRIVATE COLLECTION
PHOTO COURTESY OF DAVID FINDLAY JR. FINE ART, NYC

see page 60

years a great number of the old "Duveneck Boys" and other artist friends sought him out in Gloucester, such as Joseph DeCamp and John H. Twachtman. This influx of talent into Cape Ann due to Duveneck's presence is a significant chapter in the artistic legacy of the region. It helped establish Cape Ann as a pilgrimage site that painters of all styles felt compelled to visit at least once in their career.

The pictures that Duveneck painted around Gloucester harbor like his masterpiece *The Yellow Shed* are innovative and show a new direction for the artist in light diffusion and color application. As an artist he was still experimenting and trying to break new ground amidst the ever increasing variety of styles and techniques developing in the art world. As a man, though, he seems to have surrendered something inside. During the years he spent on Cape Ann he never exhibited his pictures, retaining nearly the entire body of work, 150 pictures, which passed directly to his son in 1919 after his death.

The loss of his wife may have devastated him to such a degree that he never recovered. It is the strange duality of a man who maintained his travels, kept teaching, surrounded himself with fellow artists and continued to produce work, yet seemed to have lost the outward ambition of a painter. The artistic instinct, the innate desire to create and work with his hands and eyes was surely still in him, while something else inside, the man underneath the artist, had been dealt a blow that he endured but never overcame.

THEODORE WENDEL

1859 – 1932

WENDEL WAS A "Duveneck Boy" who, like his mentor, had his early training in Cincinnati. In 1879 Wendel and his friend Joseph DeCamp traveled to Munich where Duveneck and his circle were based. He spent the next two years in Germany and Italy with the group. Unlike many of Duveneck's protegés, Wendel did not become an imitator of his teacher. His style was never significantly changed by Duveneck's darker, "Munich" palette. The greatest artistic influence on Wendel occurred when he visited Giverny in 1887 and was profoundly impressed with Monet's work. Along with fellow artists like John Leslie Breck, Wendel became one of the first Americans to adopt Impressionism.

Wendel returned to America in 1889 and shortly thereafter made his first trip to Cape Ann as a teacher. In 1892 Wendel's first pictures of the region were exhibited in Boston in a show with Theodore Robinson. By the 1890's Wendel was teaching in Boston at the Cowles Art School and at Wellesley College. In 1897, Wendel married and after a honeymoon in Europe he and his wife returned and moved to Ipswich.

Like Monet in Giverny, whose lifestyle in the country Wendel so admired, he saw in Ipswich a place where he could make his roots and his future body of work. At Giverny Wendel had recognized in Monet a sublime intimacy between the artist and his surroundings. The French master had created a world around him that, for a bohemian expatriate like Wendel, seemed to be the greatest achievement for a painter: to discover and establish roots in a beautiful region, to capture its light and color, and to become a product of its beauty while making it his own.

In 1899 Wendel and his wife Philena found such a place on a farm in Ipswich which his wife had inherited from her father. Wendel often kept company with friends from Europe like Duveneck, DeCamp and Robinson. Wendel passed the next several years working in Ipswich and around Cape Ann, painting many diverse aspects of the region, including people, landscapes and harbor pieces. His shows in Boston were well received.

Many critics believed Wendel's best work was produced in these years on Cape Ann. By that time Wendel had worked past his initial exposure to Monet and had developed his own original Impressionistic style in both pastel and oils, like *Gloucester Yacht Club*. The large sailing vessel in the background is an immediate indication of the era in which it was painted, in an otherwise timeless image of the Cape Ann coast. The colors are mellowed yet are still strong, contrasting and vibrant. The multiple balcony planted on rocks near the shore is very characteristic of the region.

Wendel worked intensely until 1917 when a prolonged illness stifled his abilities. Though he lived until 1932, health complications largely ended his artistic career in the late teens. He died in Ipswich.

Summertime
1895 PASTEL ON PAPER 22" X 26"
GOLDFIELD GALLERIES

Gloucester Yacht Club
CA. 1895 OIL ON CANVAS 25" X 30"
PRIVATE COLLECTION
PHOTO COURTESY OF VOSE GALLERIES OF BOSTON

CHILDE HASSAM

1859 – 1935

CHILDE HASSAM made several trips to Cape Ann over his career, perhaps more than any of the other major American Impressionists. Hassam traveled widely over his lifetime, from Cuba to Maine and all over Europe. Constantly moving about, Hassam's work from each period produced legends; but New England and specifically the North Shore had a particular appeal which grew more acute over his lifetime. His visits to Cape Ann coincide with every major period in his artistic development, from his pre-Impressionist days, through his stays at Old Lyme in the Florence Griswold home, to his monumental series of flag pictures in New York around the First World War.

There is still some dispute over when Hassam's first visit to Cape Ann occurred. Some sources note that in 1880 or possibly 1881 Hassam made his first trip to Gloucester when still in his early twenties. He had not yet traveled to Europe, and it would not be until his second trip to France that he would embrace Impressionism. Hassam had been making a living illustrating for children's stories and studied with Ignatz Marcel Gaugengigl. His early work was tonal, bearing the Barbizon influence of the times. In 1883, Hassam traveled to France, studying at the Académie Julian. He again visited France in 1886, and at this time his techniques became more Impressionistic. After a three year stay, Hassam

Old Granite Pier, Rockport
1919 WATERCOLOR 15" X 22"
COLLECTION OF THE ROCKPORT ART ASSOCIATION

Gloucester Harbor
1899 OIL ON CANVAS 24 1/2" X 22 1/2"
PRIVATE COLLECTION
PHOTO COURTESY OF SPANIERMAN GALLERY, LLC

returned to America and the following year, in 1890, he returned to Gloucester for the summer. Working in both watercolor and oil, his work was now colorful, lighter and dazzling to the eye.

His visits now became more frequent. Returning for five of the seven summers between 1894 and 1900, Hassam's trips took on a richer significance. His prolonged trips to high profile places in Europe and the Mediterranean had perhaps forced Hassam to contemplate America and what it meant to be an American. As Jay E. Cantor describes:

"(Hassam's) visits to Portsmouth, Gloucester... provided opportunities for him to reclaim his patrimony and assert his Americanness at a time of expanding foreign incursions. Hassam's response to these historical communities was determined in part by their own character but also influenced by what became his infatuation with the idea of the colonial as the essential expression of American character. The colonial existed not only in the history of these old towns and in their surviving buildings but also in the very sense of place." [9]

Like his church pictures from Old Lyme, Hassam had a great fondness for the churches in Cape Ann, especially the First Unitarian Church in Gloucester. He also painted the streets, shipbuilding yards and the harbors. Painted in 1899, *Gloucester Harbor* is one of Hassam's most well-known Cape Ann pictures. Hassam loved the harbor, and like many of his fellow Impressionists, was continuously intrigued with the view of the harbor from Banner Hill. Today heralded as a Master Impressionist, Hassam strangely disapproved of the label and resisted it throughout his life. Though his works are Impressionistic, he never totally eliminated form for pure color; as in *Gloucester Harbor* the structural integrity of the landscape remains, indicative of the traditional realism that Hassam never abandoned. The view from Banner Hill enabled Hassam to compress the depth of field into a series of flat plains; the result is a signature skyline that has perhaps become the Motif #1 of Gloucester, an icon.

By 1905, Hassam was painting in Old Lyme, and by 1916 was working on his "Flag Series" in New York. Up until the year of his death Hassam remained active, crisscrossing New England for a variety of painting trips and exhibitions. From these travels and layover stops en route to Maine, Hassam returned to Gloucester in 1915, 1916, 1918, and in 1919 he stayed from July until September in Gloucester and Rockport.

The Church at Gloucester
1918 ETCHING 13 3/4" X 10 1/2"
COLLECTION OF MR. AND MRS. WILLIAM TRAYES

(OPPOSITE)
Ten Pound Island
1896 OIL ON CANVAS 32 1/8" X 32 1/4"
JACK WARNER FOUNDATION, TUSCALOOSA, AL
PHOTO COURTESY OF HIRSCHL & ADLER GALLERIES, INC.

JOHN LESLIE BRECK
1860 - 1899

JOHN LESLIE BRECK'S tragic death from gas inhalation at the age of 39 while sleeping saw the passing of a man that John Twachtman credited with bringing Impressionism to America. He was one of the first Americans to work in Giverny and was so taken by the beauty of the region and the kindness of the locals that he was determined to make the place known to other artists. Breck had been born at sea in the Pacific off the coast of Guam and was brought to Boston by his mother after the death of his father, a sea captain. While studying in Munich at the Royal Academy he met artists like Theodore Wendel and Joseph DeCamp. Breck spent four years painting in New England before traveling to France in 1886 to attend the Académie ·Julian which led to his exposure to Monet in Giverny. Breck's works from this period onwards are bold, vivid pictures that require no further proof that Breck was one of the best of the American Impressionists.

Breck's return to the United States in the early 1890's saw a new era for the painter. He traveled widely, even visiting California, but spent a majority of his time until his death around the Massachusetts coast. Many of Breck's Cape Ann paintings as well as his Giverny pictures were exhibited at the St. Botolph Club in Boston. By the late 1890's Breck had shed the vestiges of his earlier Tonalism and his Impressionism had an even more confident style and a delicacy of color and light suggesting spectacular works in the years ahead. Many of his paintings of ponds and the countryside around Cape Ann could almost be mistaken for Giverny if not for the stunning blue sea found on the horizon.

Breck painted throughout Annisquam, Gloucester and Ipswich. His work became more bright and more panoramic than his European pictures, reflecting the open sky and elevated views of Cape Ann, compared to the often enclosed, insular quality of Giverny. As Dr. William Gerdts describes one of Breck's Annisquam pictures in *Lasting Impressions* , "In such works, Giverny and Impressionism had effectively been transferred to America."[10]

Some reminiscences describe Breck as a melancholy man who was often unable to find the outward ambition to have made a bigger name for himself while fellow painters around him garnered more and more accolades. But his death from gas asphyxiation from an open vent was by no means an uncommon accident at the time. His early death sealed an often obscured and unsung place in the history of American Impressionism.

Lynn Shanties, Essex River
CA. 1890'S OIL ON CANVAS 18" X 22"
PRIVATE COLLECTION
PHOTO COURTESY OF BROWN CORBIN FINE ART

Near Annisquam, Autumn
CA. 1894 OIL ON CANVAS 45 1/8" X 46 1/2"
PRIVATE COLLECTION
PHOTO COURTESY OF BROWN CORBIN FINE ART

ERIC HUDSON
1864 – 1932

THE FIRST TIME Hudson visited Rockport, he came by boat. Living in Boston, he grew up on the water and used to sail to the North Shore region with friends. Though Hudson is most known for his association with Monhegan Island, his career as a marine painter took him to waters from New England to Scandinavia to the Caribbean, often returning to Rockport throughout his life.

Hudson's love for art and for the water began in his early years as did his fascination with the harbors of Rockport. In the 1880's, after some study with Marshall Johnson in Boston, he ventured to Paris where he trained at the Académie Julian. In the 1890's Hudson was back in Rockport, sometimes in the company of Parker Perkins, at a time when relatively few artists were to be seen in the town. Hudson's seafaring abilities most likely intensified his come-and-go tendencies. He studied the works of painters throughout Europe, but he is still regarded as a largely self-taught painter. Royal Cortissoz describes his work as "...acquainted with the old masters but saturated in a sturdy Americanism."[11] His work reveals a style developed while painting on small boats and isolated islands rather than from salons or under renowned masters.

Hudson often painted from a small dory in the water. From such a low perspective, he created images that present things in bulk form, lending a massiveness to the vessels in pictures such as *The Tug*. Other pictures like *The Dorymen* also lend this sense of closeness that produces very Expressionistic effects. In 1918, he and his family lived for the whole summer on his boat "Anchorage," docked in Rockport harbor. Hudson is said to have had close friendships with fishermen wherever he went. Perhaps, like them, he was truly more at home on the water. In the early morning hours when sketching their boats they would often delay departure until he had completed his drawing.

Later he moved into a home on the shore, the "Hannah Jumper" house on 35 Mt. Pleasant Street. He painted a great variety of Cape Ann subject matter: shorelines, surf, fishermen, ship building yards and around the small islands off the coast. A member of the North Shore Art Association and the Rockport Art Association, Hudson had friendships with painters like George Bellows and Robert Henri and fellow marine painter Frederick Waugh. He died in Rockport, overlooking the harbor from his home.

It is said that his favorite quote was:

"I must down to the seas again
To the lonely sea and the sky
And all I ask is a tall ship
And a star to steer her by" [12]

Ships Passing
1890 OIL ON CANVAS 12" X 20"
PRIVATE COLLECTION

The Dorymen
CA. 1930'S OIL ON CANVAS 28" X 34"
PRIVATE COLLECTION

The Tug
CA. 1930'S OIL ON CANVAS 28 1/2" X 34"
PRIVATE COLLECTION

YARNALL ABBOTT
1870 – 1938

ABBOTT HAD AN unusual education for a painter: a law degree. He went on to pursue his studies of law at the University of Pennsylvania Law School and set up a practice in Philadelphia with his father. He wrote essays on the arts for the Encyclopedia Britannica and was also a musician, playing the organ at church services. He also pursued his own aspirations in painting with studies at the Pennsylvania Academy of Fine Arts where he trained under Thomas Anshutz. Later he traveled to Paris where he was taught by Gustave Courtois and Louis Raphael Collin.

Like many other artists, Abbott summered in Rockport while spending winters elsewhere. He settled in Philadelphia but always returned to Cape Ann where he most enjoyed painting harbor and coastal scenes. Like fellow painters such as Antonio Cirino, Abbott's interests in the arts and learning covered many diverse fields beyond the easel. He wrote articles for magazines and was an avid traveler. He also became a lecturer on art and art appreciation, often stressing the importance that Americans buy American art.

Despite Abbott's other scholarly pursuits, and regardless of his travels, he was always enamored with the New England tableau. The houses and streets in the small towns along the coast were the inspiration for his pictures. Painted in the summer of 1927, *Fishermen's Houses* illustrates this love for the quaint and simple beauty of the homes that hug the rocky coast of towns like Rockport. Nestled in a little inlet, the cozy homes resting on wood pilings, jutting out over the water have been a staple image of Cape Ann and a constant source of interest and fascination for outsiders and painters alike. The picture has a subdued quality, heavy with shadows and dark spaces yet is still filled with pastel shades of color, lending a gentle, village atmosphere.

Abbott made great use of his legal background by personally drafting the by-laws and constitution for the Rockport Art Association at its founding and served as President in 1924 and 1925.

Fishermen's Houses
1927 OIL ON CANVAS 30 1/8" X 36 1/8"
PRIVATE COLLECTION
PHOTO COURTESY OF THE SCHWARZ GALLERY

WILLARD LEROY METCALF
1858 - 1925

WHEN METCALF was still a small boy, his parents, believing in the occult, took part in a séance in which a spirit from another world, apparently named "Caravaggio" or "Correggio," informed them that their son would become a celebrated painter "when the snow of winter lay upon his brow."[13] His parents very quickly started their son taking art lessons. Metcalf became a founding member of the now legendary Ten American Painters. However, unlike many of his peers, Metcalf's evolution was slow. He was not an immediate artistic prodigy at 25 like Hassam or Chase; he spent many years experimenting, changing his style, while working as an illustrator, struggling to find a voice that most corresponded to his nature.

Born in Lowell, Massachusetts, Metcalf had early training at the Lowell Institute then at the School of the Museum of Fine Arts in Boston. Documenting the life of the Zuni Indians from 1881–1883, he then went to France where he studied at the Académie Julian. At this stage, Metcalf's style was a dark, Barbizon-influenced palette. Though Metcalf was one of the first Americans to visit Monet at Giverny, he was not a quick convert to Impressionism. His style remained conservative and more traditional upon his return to New York. Mysteriously, Metcalf did have a brief interlude with pure impressionism then abandoned it for almost a decade before returning again, fully dedicated, to the impressionist vision. That interlude occurred in Gloucester.

Metcalf most likely came to Cape Ann on the advice of his friend Childe Hassam. Some sources suggest Metcalf visited the area as early as 1890, but it was his documented arrival with Hassam in 1895 that produced a turning point and a glimpse of things to come. Until then, Metcalf had been a portrait painter, teacher and illustrator. His Gloucester pictures that summer were his first American landscapes in years. Exposure to Hassam's work and the light and color of Cape Ann ignited a dormant aesthetic energy that had remained latent in Metcalf's earlier work.

Metcalf was suddenly producing work like *Gloucester Harbor*. The image bears little evidence of his conservative approach, while the color and unusual perspective represent a major innovation

Bickford's Float, Smith's Cove, Rocky Neck
1899 OIL ON CANVAS 13 1/8" X 16"
COLLECTION OF ROBERT SCHWARZ, PHILADELPHIA

(OPPOSITE)
Gloucester Harbor
1895 OIL ON CANVAS 26" X 28 3/4"
MEAD ART MUSEUM, AMHERST COLLEGE
GIFT OF GEORGE D. PRATT
CLASS OF 1893

in the attitude of the painter. Metcalf's impressionistic technique is still controlled yet hints at the looser, broken color style he would refine so elegantly in the years ahead. Upon Metcalf's return to New York, a variety of commission work and mural painting consumed his energy, thus halting further exploration into Impressionism.

In 1904, in an exhibition of some of his pictures, Metcalf described a Renaissance that had occurred in his work. Reverting to his brief encounter with Impressionism, Metcalf once again began to work in brighter color and broken brush work in outdoor settings. His popularity increased as did sales, commissions and his celebrity in New York and Boston. Metcalf's brief exposure to Gloucester in 1895 revealed his future direction, a future for which he was perhaps still not ready. It would take another ten years of working to bring him back to that place. His time in Gloucester was brief, but like many great artists who came to Cape Ann, the region had more effect on his work than he had upon the region.

Like the prophecy his parents heard, Metcalf had become a renowned painter in his mid-forties, his hair greyed, "when the snow of winter lay upon his brow."

EDWARD POTTHAST

1857 – 1927

TODAY, Edward Potthast is most remembered for his stunning beach scenes of bathers by the shore and the startling effects of reflected sunlight. He had an affinity for these pictures and produced many of them, as though they offered him a form of meditation. However, examining Potthast's career one sees an incredible diversity of styles, techniques and disciplines of far greater range than found in most other painters of his day. Potthast's "modified impressionism," apparent in such pieces as his beach scenes, was not born of a gifted spontaneity, but was the product of years of work and study in many facets of commercial and fine art.

Born in Cincinnati, Potthast was raised in the city that produced other great artists like Duveneck. It took Potthast much longer than most of his contemporaries to generate the funds to travel to Europe and enjoy the many fineries of expatriate, artistic life. Having studied at the McMiken School of Design and later at the University of Cincinnati Art Department, he worked for several years as an illustrator and lithographer before finally having the funds to go to Europe, studying in Antwerp in 1880 and Munich in 1884. He later returned for a number of years to study in Paris in the early 1890's where he pursued many different styles from the traditional Barbizon to the Impressionistic, creating such a diverse body of work that often viewers do not believe they were rendered by the same hand.

Potthast eventually settled in New York in 1895 and was often in the company of painters like Duveneck and Twachtman. It was most likely through these contacts that he learned of Cape Ann which he first visited in 1896. For the next twenty years he spent his summers there, always at the shore or harbor, finding the diversity of fishermen, pleasure seekers and the landscape itself a natural muse for his vision. While many of

Gloucester Harbor
CA. 1910 OIL ON CANVAS 25" X 30"
PRIVATE COLLECTION
PHOTO COURTESY OF KENNETH LUX GALLERY

At the Beach
CA. 1915 OIL ON CANVAS 16 1/4" X 20 1/4"
PRIVATE COLLECTION
PHOTO COURTESY OF KENY GALLERIES

his stunning harbor pictures are easily identifiable because of obvious land marks and scenery, it is difficult to establish which of his seaside pictures were done in Cape Ann compared to Coney Island or other beaches. Potthast rarely identified the location of any of his pictures. He seemed to enjoy the more ambiguous depiction of general life at the shore.

Historians have had difficulty reconstructing much of his life in any great detail. Potthast's own quiet demeanor and the absence of any diaries have left many gaps in his life for tracing the changes in his style. He seems to have been a somewhat puzzling man even for his contempo-raries, as described in a well-known quote by his friend Henry Farny,

"If the man was not so infernally modest and allowed me to send some of his stuff to the World's Fair you would have heard a good deal more about him by this time. But no he said they were only 'sketches' and I couldn't get the idiot to let them go."[14]

He is remembered as being very quiet, preferring to listen than to speak. He was also known to have rarely, if ever, been totally pleased with any picture he painted. This seems peculiar and perhaps sad for a man who has been regarded as the "Master of the Beaches."

CECILIA BEAUX

1855 — 1942

IN 1899, at an awards ceremony, William Merritt Chase pronounced Cecilia Beaux, "the greatest woman painter of modern times."15 She had earned such accolades for her accomplishments and success as a portrait painter, whose subjects over her career included Theodore Roosevelt and Henry James. Beaux's approach to portrait painting rivaled John Singer Sargent; her images have a liveliness, a great range of color and fluid, lush brushwork that invigorated the portrait genre.

Born in Philadelphia, Beaux showed early artistic talent in drawing and was encouraged by her grandparents, who raised her. First taking lessons in Philadelphia, she developed an early fondness for rendering the likeness of others' faces. She also worked in etching and lithography, challenged by the fact that a single mistake would show. Training under William Sartain, Beaux was determined to make practical and economic use of her skills. She won the Mary Smith Prize in 1887 at the Pennsylvania Academy of Fine Arts and by 1888 traveled to Paris to study at the Académie Julian. Winning great acclaim for a portrait at the 1889 Paris Salon, the direction of her career seemed to be set.

Returning to America in 1890, Beaux's career as a portrait painter seldom lacked for commissions. Never marrying, she concentrated on her career and slowly moved into the high society of those she painted. In 1890, Beaux became the first woman appointed as a full-time teacher at the Pennsylvania Academy of Fine Arts. By the late 1890's she had made her first visits to Gloucester. Beaux may have first heard of Cape Ann through the artist Stephen Parrish who occupied a studio across the hall from her own while in Philadelphia in the late 1880's. Beaux was profoundly inspired by Parrish's life, his encouragement and kind words, not to mention his great skill in etching.

By 1905, Beaux had built a house and studio on Eastern Point, dubbed "The Green Alley," for the landscaped path that led to her front door. So sought after was she that individuals traveled to Gloucester in order to sit for her, sometimes seeking temporary residence in the region until the sessions were completed. Thus Cape Ann became better known among the growing wealthy class, who were frequently her clients. Often sitters would stay in her adjoining guesthouse.

Painted in 1902, *Man with a Cat* is actually a portrait of Henry Sturgis Drinker, husband of Cecilia's sister, Etta. Several of the Drinker family would sit for Beaux over the years. Dominated by white and cream colors Beaux still managed to convey a startling array of textures and sharp contrasts of light and shadow. Drinker was a determined, energetic lawyer. Such men often had their portraits painted. Such men, however, were not always the best subjects for producing truly sumptuous paintings. But in Beaux's hands, the picture becomes a luscious image of brushwork with shots of vibrant color. Rather than conforming to the whims of a demanding sitter, Beaux delivers an image which has become much more than a portrait of a lawyer. Dressed in a summer suit, with windows and shutters open to the air, it is a lively, refreshing image.

A broken hip sustained after a fall in 1924 left Beaux crippled. It so limited her mobility that she eventually ceased to paint, but she turned to writing her memoirs with equal energy. She continued to receive many awards until the end of her life, including the National Achievement Gold Medal given to her by Eleanor Roosevelt. She died in her home in Gloucester.

(OPPOSITE)
Man with a Cat
(Portrait of Henry Sturgis Drinker)
1902 OIL ON CANVAS 48" X 34"
COLLECTION OF THE SMITHSONIAN AMERICAN ART
MUSEUM, BEQUEST OF HENRY WARD RANGER
THROUGH THE NATIONAL ACADEMY OF DESIGN 1952.10.1

JOHN TWACHTMAN
1853 - 1902

TWACHTMAN'S pictures of Cape Ann were created at the end of a career about which art historians of today still have differing opinions. In reading about his life and career from source to source one finds continuous contradictions about his personality, and the perception of his importance in American Art.

Born in Cincinnati, Twachtman began his artistic life with Frank Duveneck at the Cincinnati School of Design, forming a lasting friendship that shaped many of the stages of Twachtman's career. In 1875, Twachtman followed Duveneck to Munich and in later years taught in Florence and studied at the Académie Julian in Paris. A founding member of The Ten in 1897, Twachtman was for many years a leading exponent of the darker, tonal Munich style. Later he was one of the first American painters to bring Impressionism to the U.S., creating wonderful Impressionistic pieces in Connecticut and New York in the 1880's and 1890's when Americans were still critical of this approach. Twachtman was always open to the influence of other styles, other schools and other artists. However, he was not an imitator; on the contrary he was continuously searching, striving for different modes of expression.

Such painters are difficult to categorize for art historians; such qualities also make it hard to garner a loyal clientele. Twachtman's pictures did not sell well in his lifetime. Despite his prolific years abroad and the landmark importance of forming The Ten, many say that when Twachtman came to Gloucester in 1900 his lack of critical praise and financial success had left him an embittered, tired man. Other biographies read quite differently, describing Twachtman as deeply in love with nature and that his time in Gloucester in the sun, by the sea, was a logical and peaceful extension of his years in the tranquility of Connecticut.

What is not disputed, however, is the vivid changes in Twachtman's style during his years on Cape Ann. Twachtman had sometimes confided to friends that he believed he had been overtrained. His Gloucester pictures seemed more concerned with spontaneity, emotion and energy than with a premeditated, academic approach based upon any style at all. Most characteristic of these last pictures is precisely the feeling that he was shedding himself of all he had previously learned. Similar to the early years of Impressionism, this new approach was once again too bold a departure, too different for critics or buyers to immediately understand. He stripped away much of the bold color of the Impressionists and sought a looser, sketchier style. Once again, some critics have described this change as impatient, hinting at Twachtman's awareness of his own impending death. Others see this as a wonderful mark of an ever-evolving artist.

Fish Sheds, Gloucester
CA. 1901 OIL ON CANVAS 25" X 30"
PRIVATE COLLECTION
PHOTO COURTESY OF SPANIERMAN GALLERY LLC

Little Giant
CA. 1900–1902 OIL ON CANVAS 20" X 24"
PRIVATE COLLECTION
PHOTO COURTESY OF SPANIERMAN GALLERY LLC

The fact remains, however, that Twachtman had already begun to explore elements of what would be called Post-Impressionism when Impressionism itself was just gaining broad acceptance in America. His Gloucester pictures do have a quality of being stripped bare, being characteristic of no school or style extant. He was also one of the first painters to embrace rather than avoid the elements of Industrialism popping up in the ports, such as steam ships and steel machinery. His choice to interpret and capture these point to the birth of the Ash Can school and later Twentieth century styles. However, his early death has left a question mark on the motives of these last years of Twachtman's life—if they were deliberate and calculated or the subconscious, natural evolution of a probing mind, if they were the desperate attempts of a man who sensed the end coming or the new aspirations of an artist with many years ahead of him. His death at forty-nine has left these questions a mystery. He is buried in Oak Grove cemetery in Gloucester.

GEORGE L. NOYES

1864 - 1954

NOYES FIRST came to the Cape Ann region in 1900. He set up residence and began to teach in Annisquam where, as the story-legend goes, a young N.C. Wyeth was one of his first students. Noyes is regarded today as one of the finest Impressionists of the Boston School, notable for his ability to capture and render sunlight and its effects on the tone and color of landscapes and water. His artistic career was marked by many years of success but also troubles and loss.

Born to American parents in Ontario, the Noyes family later relocated to New England where George began art training with George Bartlett at the Massachusetts Normal School. Later after abandoning an apprenticeship for a career in glass design at the New England Glass Company, Noyes traveled to Paris in 1890 where he studied under Gustave Courtois and Joseph-Paul Blanc. In Blanc's atelier Noyes befriended Maurice Prendergast. It was during his European travels that he developed his skill for plein air painting. In 1892 Noyes traveled to Algeria and then to Italy where he met up with his brother Edward, an accomplished pianist studying in Dresden. In 1893 Noyes set up a studio in Boston and began to exhibit his pictures with his friend Prendergast and others.

Later in 1897 Noyes had the great fortune to join an aging Frederic Edwin Church on a trip to Mexico where they traveled and painted together. Noyes' role seems to have been that of an assistant, an apprentice and a student. This exposure certainly contributed to Noyes' sense of respect for the landscape and remaining truthful to its basic elements.

Upon returning to New England, Noyes' roots became firmly planted in Boston and the North Shore region. He began to exhibit at the Boston Art Club and the Boston Society of Watercolor. Thereafter, Noyes began to explore the countryside of Massachusetts, painting throughout Canton, Medfield, Cape Cod and North Hampton before his journeys finally brought him to Cape Ann. After settling in Annisquam, Noyes began to work with Eric Pape, who directed many young artists to his instruction, including N.C. Wyeth, who once wrote in a letter, "I am arranging to study a part of my time with George Noyes. His color knowledge is superb and I think he will give me much help at this juncture."16

The Yellow Shed from Banner Hill
CA. 1920'S OIL ON PANEL 14" X 14"
PRIVATE COLLECTION
PHOTO COURTESY OF DAVIES FINE ARTS
see page 37, 84

Yawl in Gloucester Harbor
CA. 1920'S OIL ON CANVAS 25" X 30"
PRIVATE COLLECTION
PHOTO COURTESY OF DAVIES FINE ARTS

Later in 1903 Noyes took a post teaching at Stanford University but continued to spend his summers on Cape Ann. While living in the San Francisco area, the Great Earthquake of 1906 destroyed nearly all of Noyes' personal possessions. He would later return to Massachusetts where he divided his time between stays in Boston and in Annisquam. The first two decades of the twentieth century proved to be the zenith for Noyes. His mature style captured the essence of broken color brushwork, well represented in *The Yellow Shed* and the breathtaking *Yawl in*

Gloucester Harbor. He was honored at the Panama-Pacific Exposition of 1915 and had several shows, enjoying critical acclaim and commercial success. He achieved great popularity in Boston among buyers, patrons and the art circles. But by the 1930's his status had wained considerably with the ever changing popularity of style with which the aging artist was out of touch.

Noyes later moved to Vermont where he continued to paint. But in 1939 a fire destroyed his studio and it is said that a great body of his life's work was lost in the flames.

WALTER HARRISON CADY

1877 - 1970

FOR LOCALS, artists and readers, Harrison Cady was best known as "the bug painter." For almost fifty years he illustrated children's books including the characters of Peter Rabbit, Jimmy Skunk and Reddy the Fox. He became a unique and colorful figure in Rockport, active in many facets of the community.

As a young man, while working for an advertising agency in New York, a friend of Cady's father took him on a car trip along the Massachusetts coast. While the gentleman was looking for witches in Salem, he was struck by the beauty of the coastal communities. A popped tire led them to a repair shop in Rockport, and after a brief stroll around the harbor, Cady decided he would have to return. He set up a studio by 1900 and befriended Parker Perkins, often sketching with him in his studio. A break came for Cady when in 1907 he began doing illustration work for Life magazine. By 1911 he was illustrating for children's books through Thornton Burgess. His father had been a nature lover and had taken young

Harrison for many field trips while growing up. Cady had great enthusiasm and energy and thus began a career that spanned many decades, creating famous characters known throughout America. Friends reminisced about entering his studio and hearing the artist talking to his animal friends on paper as he rendered them.

Cady maintained his illustration work while painting the local scenery and working in community events, auctions and charities. When he was in his seventies he finally put down his illustrator's pen and worked purely on his own art. As can be seen from his picture *Lane's Cove* he was a talented landscape painter but still retained a childlike purity of essence. His years as one of the most beloved artists in the country for children and parents had brought him great joy as an artist, as had all his other endeavors as an artist, as he once said to a friend, "It's funny the amount of work a fellow turns out in a lifetime. First it was beetles and rabbits and crickets, then mountains, then nudes, then priests and bishops. They all interest me."[17]

Lane's Cove
CA. 1950 OIL ON BOARD 20" X 30"
PRIVATE COLLECTION

Essex Boat Yard
CA. 1950 OIL ON BOARD 25" X 30"
PRIVATE COLLECTION

FREDERICK J. MULHAUPT
1871 – 1938

MULHAUPT IS REGARDED as one of the finest artists to work on Cape Ann, a member of the "imported" group who were not indigenous to Massachusetts nor the greater New England area. Despite Mulhaupt's distant origins in the Midwest where he spent many years before traveling, he is regarded as "the Dean of the Cape Ann School."

Born in Rock Port, *Missouri*, Mulhaupt's early years were spent around the Kansas-Missouri border region, sometimes in areas still viewed as "Indian country." His first career-oriented job was with a magazine in the now legendary Dodge City. But a change in aspirations eventually found him taking courses at the Kansas City School of Design. By the early 1890's Mulhaupt had made his way to Chicago, at the time the only place of opportunity for aspiring artists in the Midwest, studying at the Art Institute. Mulhaupt spent many years in Chicago, helping to found the Chisel and Palette Club and eventually becoming a teacher at the Art Institute. By 1904 he had made the leap and settled in New York, joining the Salmagundi Club.

However, like many budding young American painters, Mulhaupt's most important decision was to study in France. Little is known of his stay or the exact itinerary of his travels, but surviving pictures from France and England, especially St. Ives, mark a new era for the painter. These were the first hints of his remarkable aptitude for coastal and harbor images, laying the foundation for his years in Cape Ann.

Hailing from Gloucester
CA. 1920'S OIL ON CANVAS 30" X 40"
PRIVATE COLLECTION
PHOTO COURTESY OF GODEL & CO., FINE ARTS

(OPPOSITE)
The Green Boat
CA. 1920'S OIL ON PANEL 12" X 16"
PRIVATE COLLECTION
PHOTO COURTESY OF DAVIES FINE ARTS

Schooner Imperator
CA. 1920'S OIL ON PANEL
12" X 16"
PRIVATE COLLECTION
PHOTO COURTESY OF
DAVIES FINE ARTS

(OPPOSITE)
Winter Quiet
CA. 1920'S OIL ON CANVAS
34" X 28"
PRIVATE COLLECTION
PHOTO COURTESY OF
VOSE GALLERIES

Upon returning to the United States, Mulhaupt took his first trip to Gloucester in 1907. His technique had matured considerably in the previous years, and in the harbors of Cape Ann he found a visual tableau of light, color and texture that he had been waiting for all of his life, as he had once described that Gloucester "duplicates any views I care to paint."[18] From then on, Mulhaupt spent most of his summers in the region, exhibiting at the Gallery-on-the-Moors in five of the first seven exhibitions. He was also a founding member of the North Shore Arts Association. By 1923, no other areas could lure Mulhaupt away, and he settled in Gloucester, eventually buying a former blacksmith's shop on Rocky Neck where he painted year round, despite the lack of running water in the winter.

Unlike many of his contemporaries, Mulhaupt was not a plein air painter, despite the spontaneous, on location style of many of his larger pictures. He was a very careful, methodical artist who did highly detailed sketches outdoors, returning to his studio where a majority of his larger pictures were produced. Few of his contemporaries were as skilled in complex compositions and subtleties of color, especially in capturing the myriad of whites and greys characteristic of his winter harbor scenes.

Although he had the deepest respect of his students who recall his encouraging style of instruction, always critiquing but never altering their canvases, they also remember him as being a very quiet, perhaps introverted man who preferred painting alone to socializing in artists' circles. He was from a more traditional, conservative era of American painters who preferred hard work rather than its symbols. Often business dealings and the sale of his pictures were left to his wife; he was too consumed by the thought of his next creation. As Charles Movalli describes Mulhaupt:

"He's like a host of other fine American painters who painted and moved on, leaving a newspaper obituary behind them. They were independent entrepreneurs, men and women who wanted to paint and who cultivated nature rather than dealers and public relations men."[19]

FREDERICK J. WAUGH

1 8 6 1 — 1 9 4 0

"FREDDY, YOU WILL never make a business-man. You will do much better as an artist."[20] Such was the advice of Frederick Waugh's father, an accomplished painter himself, to the young man who would do more to popularize pure marine painting than any other American artist of his day. Such encouragement led Frederick, aged nineteen, to study at the Pennsylvania Academy of Fine Arts under the guidance of Thomas Eakins. In 1883 Waugh went to study at the Académie Julian in Paris, but it was during a trip to England that Waugh began to study the sea, observing it for hours, determined to develop new techniques to capture the movement and drama of crashing surf. He remained in England until 1907, and while working as an illustrator and painting along the coast he began building a reputation, selling many pictures. His gift for capturing the ocean was remarkable; no longer did he need to place a token ship on the horizon or hints of man's presence on the shoreline to aesthetically round out the painting. His ability to render what his own son later called "the true push and heave of the ancient thundering ocean"[21] was enough to fill a picture. Absent of man, the images suggest the viewer is witnessing the grand spectacle of mother nature at her very source, in all her beauty and turbulence.

Having moved back to New Jersey, Waugh abandoned commercial work and began traveling the New England coast, looking for any shoreline that might reveal another side of the ocean in all its passion and majesty. This quest led him from Provincetown to Monhegan Island and Bailey's Island. It was during this extended stay in Maine that Waugh and his wife, having exhausted the area's potential for a time, decided to go to Cape Ann, an area of which they had heard so much. Arriving in the summer of 1910, Waugh set about hunting for the drama of the shoreline and found something which changed the nature of his palette and technique. As George R. Havens describes in his biography on Waugh,

Gloucester Harbor
1910 OIL ON CANVAS 25" X 30"
PRIVATE COLLECTION
PHOTO COURTESY OF THE COOLEY GALLERY

(OPPOSITE)
Cape Ann Waters
1910 OIL ON CANVAS 10" X 14"
PRIVATE COLLECTION
PHOTO COURTESY OF DAVIES FINE ARTS

"Whether it was a belated influence of impressionism, coming to the surface suddenly after lying dormant through all these years, or only an instinctive mood of experimentation on his part, quite unconnected, consciously at least, with any artistic tendencies that had gone before, he now began to work with a thick impasto and a full use of undiluted color which reflected the vivid impact of these new scenes. In consequence, these Gloucester paintings have a shimmer, a vibration, a brilliance, which are in peculiar harmony with the subject." 22

While in Gloucester, Waugh returned to his early years in St. Ives, painting pictures of the docks and boats. He spent days venturing into Gloucester harbor in a dory, with his son Coulton on the oars, paint and canvas all around him, and he would spend the day painting different views of the harbor. Because of Waugh's unique, singular search for the drama of the ocean, once he had exhausted the possibilities of the region, he moved on, in search of more surf.

Consequently, Waugh spent only one summer on Cape Ann. However the influence that the light and color of the region had on his style is significant. His brief return to painting harbor pictures has left a small but unique body of work from the period. Most significantly, his skill popularized pure marine painting amidst a large audience, and together with his many instructional books, inspired a new, legitimate genre unto itself, the influence of which can still be seen in galleries throughout Cape Ann today.

PAUL CORNOYER

1864 — 1923

PAUL CORNOYER WAS a part of the great movement of Impressionism that took hold in France and then spread to America in the last decades of the nineteenth century. Born in St. Louis to French emigrés, Cornoyer first took art classes at the St. Louis School of Art where he came under the guidance of Halsey C. Ives. In 1889 he traveled to Paris where he studied at the Académie Julian under accomplished French artists like Jules Lefebvre and Benjamin Constant. Cornoyer studied in France for five years, an unusually long stay compared to other young artists visiting from America. This provided sufficient time for him to become mesmerized by French Impressionism. He studied and developed his own unique, conservative Impressionism as he painted in London and Venice, returning to St. Louis in 1894 where he won several important commissions.

Indirectly, it was Cornoyer's contact with William Merritt Chase that first drew Cape Ann to his attention. Impressed with the younger artist's work, Chase acquired a picture of Cornoyer's and wrote to him, urging him to move to New York, which he did in 1898. There he met artists like Twachtman and Hassam and many other painters who were very familiar with Rockport and Gloucester. He began to travel and paint in different regions of New England, especially Connecticut and Massachusetts, expanding his reputation as a fine painter and teacher. By 1915 Cornoyer was a summer regular at John Sloan's famous "Red Cottage" on East Main St. near Rocky Neck in Gloucester. Cornoyer was immortalized in a photo with Sloan, Charles and Alice Winters and others seated before the "Red Cottage." By 1917 he had set up a studio and a permanent residence in East Gloucester. The back steps of his home are captured in the painting entitled *My Studio*.

For the remaining years of his life, Cornoyer was an active member of the Cape Ann community, teaching energetically and painting throughout the region. Cornoyer was one of the founding members of the Gloucester Art Association in 1922, acting as the first vice president of the organization which would change its name only two weeks later to the North Shore Arts Association. He passed away the following year.

My Studio, East Gloucester
CA. 1918 OIL ON CANVAS 20" X 24"
PRIVATE COLLECTION
PHOTO COURTESY OF DAVIES FINE ARTS

MAX KUEHNE

1880 – 1968

MAX KUEHNE LIVED a vigorous, energetic life both in the studio and outdoors. His Impressionist style and vivid rendering of light and color were a natural development of the open air painting that he practiced for many years of his life. Born in Halle, Germany, Kuehne's family relocated to Flushing, New York in 1894. It was here that Kuehne grew to love the active, outdoor life, spending the summer months on the Hudson River swimming, rowing and sailing.

Compared with other artists of his stature, Kuehne began formal art training late in life, at the age of 27. Despite this, he had the great fortune of studying with two of the finest American painters of the time, William Merritt Chase, a member of The Ten, and Robert Henri, a leading artist of the Ashcan School. The influence on Kuehne of these two painters, these two schools—Impressionist and Realist, during his formative years of training is incalculable. They instilled in him perhaps the best values, techniques and approaches of both styles, acquiring as well a fierce independence and confidence in himself, especially from Henri with whom Kuehne sometimes exhibited in New York.

In 1910, Kuehne left to study and travel in Europe, visiting Germany, England, France, Belgium and Holland. He did most of his traveling on a bicycle, not surprising for a man who loved exercise in the outdoors. Kuehne wrestled with the many different styles and techniques he was exposed to in Europe, from Fauvism to Cubism to the Old Masters; each he studied methodically, embracing and rejecting elements as he continued training. Reflecting the continuous influence of fellow artists like Chase, Hassam, Metcalf and Twachtman, Kuehne had truly developed a mature and original approach to painting by the time he first visited Cape Ann in 1912.

Gloucester Harbor, Site of
North Shore Arts Association
1912 OIL ON CANVAS 19 1/2" X 24"
PRIVATE COLLECTION
PHOTO COURTESY OF
DAVID FINDLAY JR., INC.

Rocky Neck, Gloucester
CA. 1913 OIL ON CANVAS 24" X 30"
PRIVATE COLLECTION
PHOTO COURTESY OF DAVIES FINE ARTS
See page 37

Kuehne's travels continued. He spent three years living in Spain with his German wife, and later lived and worked in New York around painters like Hopper and Glackens. Kuehne returned to Cape Ann again in 1918, and spent every summer there beginning in 1920. He eventually established a studio on Gott St. in Rockport, formerly occupied by Jonas Lie. He maintained an active schedule, becoming something of a legend for his energetic pursuits: painting in the morning, swimming or sailing in the afternoon, then a lunch or picnic outside. Kuehne is remembered having once said that he

came to Cape Ann to paint but he stayed to sail. For a decade, he was content to maintain his independent status, before joining the Rockport Art Association in 1940. Kuehne's finest work was accomplished in the teens and twenties. He appears to have been very hard hit by the Depression years. To make ends meet he developed a career creating decorative screens, panels and furniture in gesso and silver leaf, skills he acquired while making his own frames.

His athletic pursuits helped him live a long life and invigorated his painting, infusing his marine and boating subject matter with a dynamic energy.

LEON KROLL
1884 - 1974

LIKE HIS CONTEMPORARY John Sloan, Kroll was deeply influenced by the Ashcan school, but he also had a strong interest in painting the female figure, both in classical and contemporary poses. When he first came to Cape Ann in 1912, his artistic inclinations led him in a different direction than other painters, attracting him more to the interior of the Cape, rather than to the harbors and fishing boats.

Born in New York City, Kroll had little encouragement from his father to pursue art. He worked odd jobs as a typist, a janitor, and doing mechanical drawings while studying at the Art Student's League under John H. Twachtman. By 1903 he was studying at the National Academy of Design. Later in 1908 he won a scholarship to study in France at the Académie Julian with Jean-Paul Laurens, earning great distinction in shows and exhibits. In 1910 he first met George Bellows in

New York and the two formed a lasting friendship.

In 1912 Kroll made his first visit to Cape Ann, painting in Gloucester. For the next several years, he was very active, traveling often to Europe and to the Southwest, but always returning to Cape Ann, spending roughly sixty summers in and around Gloucester. Unlike many other painters whose palettes were altered by the light and landscape of the region, Kroll seems to have adapted the environment to his own style. He often preferred inland subjects such as farmlands and quarry areas, depicting the landscape with a similar moody, darker palette like his New York paintings. This achieved a more pensive, sometimes melancholy atmosphere. There were exceptions to his modus where occasional examples seem to have been greatly affected by the sunlight and atmosphere of the Cape in the summer; these paintings are of a drastically different style and truly appear to be the work of another hand. *Good Harbor Beach* is a rare example.

Over the decades a large body of work accumulated in the recesses of Kroll's studio that was never shown or sold until around the time of his death. Subsequent exhibitions have exposed many of these works to the public.

Kroll reached the height of his popularity in the 1930's. He was commissioned to paint several murals throughout the United States, and even a mosaic on the dome at the U.S. Military Cemetary at Omaha Beach in Normandy in commemoration of the D-Day Invasion. He won numerous awards over the years, including the "Chevalier of the Legion d'Honneur" of France and he was given the President's Medal for a lifetime of distinguished service to American Art at the National Academy of Design.

Nude
CA. 1932 OIL ON CANVAS 36" X 27"
COLLECTION OF MR. AND MRS. WILLIAM TRAYES

Good Harbor Beach
1912 OIL ON CANVAS 26" X 32"
PRIVATE COLLECTION
PHOTO COURTESY OF
A.J. KOLLAR FINE PAINTINGS

Spring, Cape Ann
1939 OIL ON CANVAS 27" X 36"
PRIVATE COLLECTION
PHOTO COURTESY OF
GERALD PETERS GALLERY

EDWARD HOPPER

1882 — 1967

FEW AMERICAN painters have remained as elusive and puzzling for biographers as Edward Hopper. Driven by a different demon, his pictures explored psychological states that had rarely been handled in painting. Perhaps even more complex and turbulent was his relationship to Jo, his wife, who modeled for nearly all of his paintings. Harmonious and yet always at odds with each other, they remained together, traveling and painting, living a Spartan existence. Though many of Hopper's famous pictures were inspired by New York City, the trips the Hoppers took offered Edward the chance to meditate on his perception of the American landscape.

Failure is not a word often associated with icons, yet success came late for Hopper (he did not paint *Nighthawks* until he was almost sixty years old). He seemed to have more psychological barriers to wrestle with than other artists and was consequently slower in formulating his vision. It was during this formative period that Hopper came to Cape Ann, and what he found there changed the course of his life.

When Edward Hopper first came to Gloucester in 1912 he had not yet sold a single picture. Irritated by illustration work and disillusioned by his stagnant progress, he came in hopes of rejuvenating his productivity. Leon Kroll was also there that summer. Knowing one another from New York, the two sometimes painted together. Kroll later remembered Hopper's paintings as empty of people or activity, as silent as Hopper himself. It was Hopper's first experience with plein air painting, and he wandered the docks of Gloucester, the Italian Quarter and Annisquam. He painted only after long deliberation; Hopper was never a spontaneous painter.

The following year in New York the 1913 Armory Show proved an inspiring event for Hopper. Here he had his very first sale of a picture, coincidentally, a painting of a sailboat, executed in 1911. But his exhilaration was short lived; he did not sell another painting for ten years. From 1915 into the 1920's, Hopper concentrated on etchings and all but abandoned oils.

It was not until 1923 that Hopper would return to Gloucester. By then his etching work had established his name among buyers and had inspired him to return to oils. That summer, while walking along Bass Rocks in Gloucester, he came upon a woman who had been an acquaintance among art circles in New York. Her name was

Cemetery at Gloucester
CONTE CRAYON 14 1/2" X 21 1/4"
PRIVATE COLLECTION

Freight Cars, Gloucester
1928 OIL ON CANVAS 29 1/4" X 40 1/8"
1956.7 GIFT OF EDWARD WALES ROOT IN RECOGNITION
OF THE 25TH ANNIVERSARY OF THE ADDISON GALLERY
COPYRIGHT ADDISON GALLERY OF AMERICAN ART, PHILLIPS
ACADEMY, ANDOVER, MASSACHUSETTS. ALL RIGHTS RESERVED

Jo Nivison, the future Mrs. Hopper. Jo had visited Gloucester as a young girl and returned in search of images to paint. The two discovered a mutual love for French poetry when Edward began a line from a Verlaine poem which Jo then finished. A romance slowly formed and the two spent the summer painting throughout Annisquam, Lanesville and Gloucester. Hopper also began to use watercolors, his first use of the medium outside his commercial work. The two of them were intrigued by Our Lady of Good Voyage on Prospect St. in the Portugese Quarter. Subjects that appealed to

Hopper are best expressed in a quote:

"At Gloucester, when everyone else would be painting ships and the waterfront, I'd just go around looking at houses. It is a solid-looking town. The roofs are very bold, the cornices bolder. The dormers cast very positive shadows. The sea captain influence I guess— the boldness of ships."[23]

One of these Gloucester pictures became the second painting Hopper ever sold as a professional artist, in a show at the Brooklyn Museum.

In 1924, Edward and Jo married in New York and honeymooned back in Gloucester, staying at Mrs. Thebaud's boarding house close to Bass Rocks. The Hoppers also spent the summers of 1926 and 1928 on Cape Ann. His pictures were selling more frequently and the variety of subject matter increased to include many infrequently painted images: factories, railroad yards, church steeples and graveyards. Bewildering at first, these images have a silence that is initially unsettling, but they contain greater sensations than mere solitude. Whereas Hopper's other entries at the 1913 Armory Show had been imitations of French themes, critics in New York were now writing about Hopper having created a style that was uniquely American.

Hopper's pictures of Gloucester may have been puzzling for many viewers. Avoiding the picturesque and the obvious, Hopper's images bordered on non-art for an era that loved experiments and innovations in impressionism and abstraction. In this mysterious meditation we sense Hopper inching closer to the essence of his perception. Like many of his New York pictures that critics described as voyeuristic, as though the figures were unaware of being watched, his images of Gloucester convey the feeling that they were the one building, the one view in town where no other painter cared to look. It was as though Hopper himself stood at the edge of a crowd that was staring at a great spectacle, and instead of looking in the same direction, something lured him away and compelled him to turn around and fix his gaze on what was unseen or had been until then, unseeable. And in the glow of sunlight hitting a silent house, he recognized himself.

Gloucester Houses
CA. 1926–28 WATERCOLOR 16" X 21 3/4"
PRIVATE COLLECTION
PHOTO COURTESY OF VANCE JORDAN FINE ART

JOHN SLOAN
1871 - 1951

IT COULD BE SAID that Cape Ann had a greater effect on John Sloan than his work had upon Cape Ann. Born in Lock Haven, Pennsylvania he was raised in Philadelphia and went to Central High School where he was classmates with future artist William C. Glackens. His family having little money, he was forced from an early age to support them while simultaneously pursuing his interest in art. For many years he juggled studies at the Pennsylvania Academy of Fine Arts with day jobs at print companies, art magazines and illustration houses. He moved to New York in 1904 and joined the circle of painters who were under the teachings of Robert Henri. This group, made up of artists like William Glackens, George Luks, Everett Shinn and Sloan, among others, came to be known as The Eight. For many years Sloan concerned himself with political and social issues of urban decay and life in the city, a style dubbed the Ash Can School, while also exploring his continued interest in painting the female nude. Both pursuits brought him praise as well as criticism.

One of Sloan's greatest struggles was the lack of time he had to explore his artistic voice. The hectic life over several years of working long hours in commercial art then exploring the streets of the city looking for subjects had finally left him mentally exhausted. The notoriety the Eight had received at the Armory Show of 1913 and in other important exhibits motivated Sloan to change the structure of his life, as he wrote at the time:

"I had been dependent on waiting for the inspiration to paint a picture because I had so little leisure time to work for myself. So I decided to save up enough money to take off a few months, go to the country and work from nature, to get fresh ideas and color rhythms."[24]

The following year he moved to Gloucester where his work took an entirely new direction. Like many painters who left the cities for the Cape, Sloan's new work was a departure from the social commentary of the Ashcan School to an exploration of the natural world and the harmony

Gloucester Trolley
OIL ON CANVAS 26" X 32"
COURTESY OF CANAJOHARIE LIBRARY
AND ART GALLERY

(OPPOSITE)
Tittering Girls
1914 OIL ON CANVAS 20" X 24"
PRIVATE COLLECTION

man found in its midst. The summer months of 1914 through 1918 Sloan spent in Gloucester where he was often found in the company of other painters like Leon Kroll, Stuart Davis and Charles Winter. Sloan's modernist style took on new dimensions and a new palette with more color that was vastly different from his monochromatic New York pictures. Cheerful, brightly colored paintings like *Tittering Girls* are a celebration of light, sun and sky, devoid of social implications or commentary. In the five summers he spent on the Cape he completed over three hundred paintings, taught courses and drew greater attention to the region for his association with Henri and the famous Eight.

Sloan had a harder road to success than many of his contemporaries of a similar stature. The long years in commercial art had trained him but also frustrated and stilted his natural growth as a painter. It is said that he didn't sell his first picture until he was forty. It was his Gloucester years that invigorated him, rejuvenating his skills which he would later bring to places like Santa Fe. Memories of Sloan's personality and demeanor differ dramatically from one account to the next, but it was his love for art that kept him going, as he once said,

"The only reason I am in this profession is because it is fun."[25]

JANE PETERSON

1876 – 1965

IN THE AGE of a largely male dominated art world, Jane Peterson was a confident, independently driven, talented artist who traveled to as many places, studied under as many top teachers and sold as many pictures as any male painter. Born in Illinois, Peterson was for many years known as a New York painter due to her years of study at the Pratt Institute, under Frank Vincent Dumond.

Peterson's student years took place during the most transitory, revolutionary period in the art world, when traditional and new, controversial styles and techniques were to be found simultaneously from exhibition to exhibition. As a result Peterson's pictures reveal many influences of Impressionism, Post-Impressionism, Expressionism and Fauvism. Her own unique style began to emerge during her intensive travels in the early 1910's, painting from first light until dusk throughout Northern Europe, the Mediterranean

and North Africa. It was during this time that Peterson began to use gouache more often for finished paintings, for it was fast drying and allowed for easy transport.

Peterson's self-reliance took her from teaching posts and assignments back and forth across the Atlantic several times before the First World War. As a result of the war, Peterson, like many other artists of the era, ceased traveling abroad and began to look at her own country for places to paint. Peterson's first trip to Cape Ann came shortly after the outbreak of war, when she visited Rockport and Gloucester. By this time both her impressionistic use of oils and especially her gouache techniques had developed into an original style, though showing a strong influence from Maurice Prendergast. She spent the summers from 1914 until 1919 painting in the streets and harbors of Gloucester. The result of these years is a truly unique interpretation of the light, water

Low Tide, Gloucester
CA. 1915 OIL ON CANVAS 30" X 40"
PRIVATE COLLECTION
PHOTO COURTESY OF SHANNON'S FINE ART

Dancing Water
CA. 1920 OIL ON CANVAS 18" X 24"
PRIVATE COLLECTION
PHOTO COURTESY OF VOSE GALLERIES

and physical forms of Cape Ann, accented with elements of Art Nouveau. The powerful influence of her approach is readily apparent in the work of Felicie Waldo Howell and Eleanor Parke Custis, as well as many others.

Peterson did not marry until 1925, at the age of 50. Forced to change a lifestyle that had been many years in development, Peterson's artistic output changed almost exclusively to floral still-lifes.

Though executed with an equally innovative approach, the magic of her earlier harbor and street scenes of Cape Ann pieces was seldom created again. Peterson also rarely dated her pictures. This has left the chronology of her development difficult to track. In 1938 Peterson was awarded the "most outstanding individual of the year" award from the American Historical Society. She is only the second woman to have won this award.

HAYLEY LEVER

1876 – 1958

HAYLEY LEVER LEFT his native Australia at the age of seventeen to study art in England. Over the next several years he grew to love the boats and harbors of St. Ives, Cornwall as well as the coastal regions of Brittany during his trips to France. While in Europe he was greatly influenced by Impressionism and later by the works of Vincent Van Gogh.

Lever thrived in England, selling pictures and joining groups such as the Royal British Artists. It was only at the urging of his friend Ernest Lawson that he was persuaded to move to America, which he did in 1911. For the next few years he submerged himself in the New York circle of artists, befriending painters like George Bellows and Robert Henri. Though he exhibited consistently at the National Academy of Design, he was never associated with any particular school or group. Lever's first exposure to Cape Ann came in 1915 when he arrived in Gloucester. Like many of his fellow painters who had sojourned in Europe, Lever recognized so much of St. Ives and Brittany in the topography and harbors of Cape Ann, and summers in Gloucester became a yearly tradition. He traveled all over the New England coast from Nantucket to Nova Scotia, exploring the many possibilities of the painted seascape, but it was always to Cape Ann that he consistently returned. Lever's finest works of Cape Ann subject matter achieve an almost tactile quality, creating a 'crushed jewel' effect. These pieces virtually shimmer in light quality.

Lever was an admired teacher at the Art Students League in New York City and brought his teaching skills to his summer classes in Gloucester. It is for his influence as a teacher that he is most often cited in the wider context of American Art. Throughout the 1920's he maintained his yearly trips to Cape Ann until the constraints of the Depression forced him to sell off property. In later years he lived in Mt. Vernon, New York where he continued to paint despite poor health. He has been quoted as telling his students,

"Art is the re-creation of mood in line, form and color. If I were confined to my own back yard for the rest of my life, I'd still have more pictures in my mind than I'd have time to paint. Art is nothing but having a good time."[26]

Gloucester Harbor from Banner Hill
1913 OIL ON CANVAS 20" X 24"
PRIVATE COLLECTION
PHOTO COURTESY OF MARK LASALLE FINE ARTS

see page 60

JONAS LIE

1880 — 1940

LIKE JOHN SLOAN, Lie's style and palette were considerably lightened and became more colorful during his exposure to the Cape Ann atmosphere. In the teens and twenties, Lie was more associated with the Ash Can style for his paintings in New York and the smoke-filled, industrial settings of his pictures from the Panama Canal in 1913. He was also known for his staunch conservative viewpoint towards art and art training, and his New York subjects seem to suggest this stern, stoic attitude.

Born in Norway, Lie found his way to New York after a brief stay in Paris following the death of his father when Jonas was only twelve. In 1893 he was living in New York with his mother and began training at Cooper Union and later at the National Academy of Design. In 1906 he studied in Paris and was very inspired by Impressionism. Upon returning to America, Lie was most associated with the New York artists and their style

when he made his first trip to Cape Ann shortly before World War I. He lived and painted in Rockport for some time, departing and not returning again until the early 1930's. When he did return he moved into a studio on Bearskin Neck and later lived in the Hannah Jumper House on Mount Pleasant Street. During his years in Rockport, Lie's impressionistic style became refined as the more somber qualities of the New York period were usurped by a more vivid, bright and open approach, reflecting the elements around him. Lie's more colorful, light palette is clearly evident in *Cape Ann Street Scene* with contrasts of sunlight and shade. However touches of the Ash Can style are evident in the brooding sky.

Lie was elected President of the National Academy of Design in 1935 and was the guest of honor in 1937 at the annual ball of the Rockport Art Association.

Indian Summer
1920 OIL ON CANVAS 35 1/2" X 42 1/2"
THE CALDWELL GALLERY

Cape Ann Street Scene
1920 OIL ON CANVAS 25" X 30"
PRIVATE COLLECTION
PHOTO COURTESY OF DAVIES FINE ARTS

STUART DAVIS

1894 – 1964

STUART DAVIS WAS truly at the vanguard of American Modernism. He had grown up in the presence of art and artists, for his father was an art editor at the *Philadelphia Press*. Davis was raised in New Jersey but by 1909 was in New York City where he began instruction under Robert Henri. His first exposure to Picasso, Matisse and Van Gogh at the 1913 Armory Show was the turning point in his career. It awakened Davis to his true calling, to go beyond the limitations of representational art. Quickly abandoning many elements of his formal training, Davis found his inspiration for modernism in a most unlikely place of traditional art, for it was on Cape Ann that Davis brought his modernist visions to life.

At the invitation of his friend John Sloan, Davis arrived with his wife in Gloucester in the summer of 1915 where they took up residence in

the famous Red Cottage. So began his yearly trips to Cape Ann which continued until 1934. At first, Davis would venture out to the shores and docks with easel, paints and canvases, engaging in the great plein air tradition, but soon found this approach restricting. He would wander the area sketching intensely then combine multiple perspectives on a single canvas in the studio. Davis was very concerned with what he called "color-space coordinates." He often said his work was not abstract, explaining that all his images were based on his observations of his physical surroundings, but as Karen Wilkin explains, "Unlike Cubist works that present multiple views of single objects, Davis juxtaposes single views of multiple objects."[27]

The one element that Davis retained from his New York roots with Henri was the Ashcan painter's fascination with the frenzied activity of human life. This may perhaps be at the core of Davis' work. He was not drawn so much to the serene shores and sunny streets of Gloucester as he was to the harbors where a maze of masts, sails, ropes, and cranes could be reworked into his pictures as tapestries of modern man.

Davis exhibited at the first Gallery-on-the-Moors show in 1916 and was also present at the creation of the Gloucester Society of Artists. His visits to Cape Ann became less frequent after 1934, but many of his pictures still continued to bear a heavy influence of his exposure to Cape Ann. At a time when the effects of the First World War had drawn many American artists away from the progressive art in Europe, Davis was a pioneer of modernism in America.

Ten Pound Island
1917 OIL ON CANVAS 23" X 19"
© ESTATE OF STUART DAVIS / LICENSED BY
VAGA, NEW YORK. PHOTO COURTESY OF
SALANDER-O'REILLY GALLERIES

(OPPOSITE)
Gloucester Terrace
1916 OIL ON CANVAS 37 1/2" X 29 1/2"
COURTESY OF CURTIS GALLERIES, INC.,
MINNEAPOLIS, MN

LILIAN WESTCOTT HALE

1881 – 1963

BORN LILIAN WESTCOTT to a family in Hartford, Connecticut, Lilian's early interest in art was honed by her mother's insistence on strict, intensive training. She had the good fortune of studying with William Merritt Chase while still a teenager; it was Chase who recommended that she travel to Boston to study with Edmund C. Tarbell at the Boston Museum School. While studying there, Philip Leslie Hale became her instructor. After she was awarded her diploma in 1902, they were married.

Though his work is highly sought after today, Philip Leslie Hale had limited success in his day. Acclaimed even then for his insightful writings on art and his skills in anatomy and painting, he is said to have had some difficulty in properly amalgamating these talents into a singular, original style. Many historians believe that his wealth of wisdom and artistic theory were channeled with greater success into Lilian Westcott Hale's work; her paintings are often said to be the clearest manifestation of much of Philip Hale's philosophy and writings on art.

Hale exhibited at the Pennsylvania Academy of Fine Arts through the 1910's and 20's. She was exposed to Cape Ann because of her sister-in-law, Ellen Day Hale's Folly Cove home "The Thickets." Despite her visits with her husband Philip, her most frequent trips occurred after Philip Leslie Hale's death in 1931. After this, the sisters-in-law spent summers in Rockport, often painting together with the other many guests that visited.

Her portrait and figural work were very popular. Elected a full member of the National Academy of Design in 1931, Hale is also often acknowledged as one of the best painters of children's portraits, in capturing distinct personality and aura. *Nancy and the Map of Europe* shows the charm and subtlety that can be captured in painting little girls, which in many ways is a genre unto its own. It requires a delicate handling and appreciation of expression and mannerisms to be sublime, rather than merely cute. Perhaps dreaming of distant lands as described in a Victorian novel the girl remains seated in an endearingly proper manner. With nearly identical hair and wearing the same color dress, the little girl and the doll mimick one another, both with a book in their hand. It is simultaneously nostalgic, humorous and eerie, not being overtly one or the other. Painted in 1919, it contains all of the precision and grace of late nineteenth century painting and its academic excellence despite the fact that Hale never had the opportunity to study in the great salons of Europe, and did not visit the continent until 1963, when she was 82 years old.

Nancy and the Map of Europe
1919 OIL ON CANVAS 46 1/2" X 40 1/2"
PRIVATE COLLECTION
PHOTO COURTESY OF ALFRED J. WALKER FINE ART

THERESA BERNSTEIN

1890 – 2002

IN HER 111 YEARS, Theresa Bernstein had seen the entire progression of twentieth century American art. Her appearance at her retrospective in New York in May, 2000 brought the presence of a living historical record.

Born in Philadelphia, Theresa Bernstein attended the Philadelphia School of Design for Women, training under Henry B. Snell. Later, after travel in Europe, Bernstein moved to New York and studied with William Merritt Chase. Her previous teacher, Snell, had a studio in East Gloucester and had taught classes there in the 1910's; it may have been through him that Bernstein first learned about Cape Ann. Her work corresponded mostly to the philosophy of the Ashcan painters; she pursued images of contemporary urban life, human activity and movement.

Establishing residence in the Pilgrim House on Rocky Neck, Bernstein arrived early enough in 1916 to exhibit her work at the first show of the Gallery-on-the-Moors, held in the same year.

In 1917, Bernstein met William Meyerowitz, who at the time was forming the People's Art Guild with friends Robert Henri and George Bellows. Meyerowitz had approached her while seeking out like-minded artists for the independent organization. After marrying in 1919, Bernstein brought Meyerowitz to Gloucester, where they lived on Eastern Point. Years later, the couple moved into a home on Mount Pleasant Avenue in East Gloucester. Bernstein taught painting courses in the summer, wintering in New York, a tradition that would remain unchanged throughout the century.

Bernstein has been described as a modernist or an expressionist. Though she believed it crucial to move away from traditional, nineteenth-century art, she also rejected cubism and abstraction. Attracted to scenes of music and social activity, Bernstein loved to depict gatherings of people: whether lazy, jubilant, or hard at work. Also, like the Ashcan group, she was determined to paint life and people as she saw them, with both its joys and difficulties. As described by Patricia M. Burnham, "Color as a path to modernity for Bernstein was pure, magnetic and sometimes even lurid: local color, independent color, color as index of feeling, color as gesture, color as lyricism." 28

Self Portrait
1916 OIL ON CANVAS 34" X 25"
PRIVATE COLLECTION

Country Fair at the Hawthorn Inn
CA. 1920'S OIL ON CANVAS 40" X 50"
PRIVATE COLLECTION

WILLIAM LESTER STEVENS
1888 – 1969

BORN IN Rockport, Stevens is undoubtedly one of the best of the native painters and is often remembered for being as eccentric as he was gifted. Born into a family of ten children with little money, Stevens spent his early years working odd jobs, often outdoors, building up a resiliency to cold and snow which would later be crucial to him as a plein air painter.

Early artistic inclinations led to instruction under local artist Parker Perkins for 50 cents a lesson. At 18 he had his first pictures accepted by the National Academy of Design and won a scholarship to the Boston Museum of Fine Arts School, training under Edmund C. Tarbell. After service in World War I, Stevens had the opportunity to study in Europe for a time. Later with fellow artists Aldro Hibbard and Harry Vincent, he helped form the Rockport Art Association, acting as a chair member. Throughout the 1930's, Stevens remained in Rockport and the Cape Ann area, teaching, organizing festivals and shows

and continuously painting, almost always outdoors no matter what the weather.

Students and friends of Stevens reminisce about his peculiarities and their many tales paint the portrait of an artist with oddly endearing eccentricities: a man who tied rocks to his canvases while painting outdoors in strong wind, a man who once lit the seat of his pants on fire with his still-burning pipe when he placed it in his back pocket while completely absorbed in speaking to a group of students. Other amusing recollections of Stevens reveal a multi-faceted man who could be spotted painting the sea or the quarries, dressed in disheveled clothes like a country "character." Yet he was also well read and held strong opinions on philosophy and poetry. He seemed to regard his own work above that of all others yet was also well known to ask for advice from locals and non-artists on interesting subjects to paint. Each colorful anecdote reveals another layer of a man who loved art, who loved learning and

Flat Ledge Quarry
CA. 1920'2 OIL ON CANVAS 50" X 60"
COLLECTION OF THE TOWN OF ROCKPORT

Aee/01

Fall Landscape
1925 OIL ON CANVAS 30" X 32"
PRIVATE COLLECTION
PHOTO COURTESY OF DAVIES FINE ARTS

Four Masted Schooner at Granite Pier
CA. 1920 OIL ON CANVAS 35" X 42"
COLLECTION OF ROCKPORT NATIONAL BANK

doing, and yet was usually so absorbed in the moment, with the picture that was right in front of him that he was most often indifferent to the fate or sale of pictures he had already finished.

Stevens' versatility is evident as one views his pure landscapes, reflecting the broken color of Metcalf, or in his powerful images of the quarries and the loading of granite. His image of *Flat Ledge Quarry* reveals his talent for painting with spontaneity and gusto, with mighty, bold brushstrokes. His mural hanging in the Rockport National Bank, on the other hand, shows his great ability to capture a monumental image in a more carefully arranged composition. The image, originally painted on three panels, is a montage of the many well-known sights in Rockport, relating to the fishing industry, quarrying and art. Included are the Granite Bridge and the original building con-

structed as the offices of the Granite Co. In the foreground, with the Motif #1 as a backdrop, men working in the quarries and fishermen cleaning and sorting their catch flank either side of an artist who stands in the middle, trying to capture it on canvas. Still containing the light contrast of his other paintings, the figural work gives the picture a strong Ashcan School quality.

Stevens later moved to Conway, Massachusetts where he constructed a studio and continued to paint with the same breakneck intensity and single-mindedness that had carried him for so long. It is estimated that he completed as many as five thousand pictures in his life time. He later spent time at teaching posts both at Princeton and Boston University. It is said that he won more awards and prizes for his work than any other living American artist of the era.

see page 5

(BELOW)
Rockport Mural
1958 OIL MURAL 41 1/2" X 120"
COLLECTION OF ROCKPORT NATIONAL BANK

HARRY VINCENT

1864 — 1931

BORN IN CHICAGO, Vincent spent his boyhood years in the Midwest where an early interest in art inspired him to teach himself how to paint. Despite later trips to France and Germany where he studied and painted, Harry Vincent is considered a self-taught painter. Little is known about his life compared to many of his contemporaries, especially his earlier years before his first trip to Cape Ann in 1918. After Vincent settled in Rockport in a studio on Atlantic Avenue, he often accompanied fishermen on their trips where he would observe, sketch and paint the majestic and turbulent activity of life at sea.

Vincent is most remembered for his dynamic marine and harbor scenes in which his unique Impressionistic style evolved from an earlier tonalist-impressionist palette like *Fall Colors*, to a bold, vibrant use of color like his distinctive version of *Motif #1*. For these he won several awards over the years during exhibitions of his pieces at the National Academy of Design, the Pennsyl-

vania Academy of Fine Arts, the Salmagundi Club and the New York Watercolor Club. Vincent took part in the creation of the Rockport Art Association in 1921 after the historic meeting of artists at Aldro Hibbard's studio on June 22 of the same year. After the establishment of the Association, he was named its first acting President.

Vincent was also an accomplished builder of museum quality model ships. Despite his self-taught background and clearly independent spirit, Vincent made a significant contribution to creating a Cape Ann genre. In 1933, after his death, the Annual RAA exhibit showed examples of Vincent's work. The respected art critic of the day, A.J. Philpot, noted Vincent's work attracted the most public attention and that, except for a few close friends, his contributions had not been truly recognized. It has only been within recent years that Harry Vincent is receiving the attention he deserves.

Fall Colors
CA. 1920 OIL ON CANVAS 22" X 28"
PRIVATE COLLECTION
PHOTO COURTESY OF DAVIES FINE ARTS

see page 5

Motif #1, Rockport
CA. 1920 OIL ON CANVAS 30" X 40"
PRIVATE COLLECTION
PHOTO COURTESY OF DAVIES FINE ARTS

Wheeler's Wharf
CA. 1920 OIL ON CANVAS 25" X 30"
PRIVATE COLLECTION
PHOTO COURTESY OF DAVIES FINE ARTS

ALDRO T. HIBBARD

1886 – 1972

PLEIN AIR PAINTING, in the French sense, may be too light a term to describe the artistic activities of Aldro Hibbard. His forté was painting outdoors in the dead of winter whether on Cape Ann or in the mountains of Vermont, accompanying wood cutters on their ox-drawn sleighs. He would awake before sunrise, march miles hip deep in snow, braving twenty below zero temperatures in order to capture on canvas the delicate, fleeting beauty of dawn's light on snow.

Whether it was his passion for painting or love of baseball, Aldro Hibbard was a pure outdoorsman. Born in Falmouth, Cape Cod, Hibbard sold his first picture in the ninth grade.

Shucking scallops, selling quick sketch portraits and shifting stage props at the Boston Opera House, he worked his way through the Massachusetts Normal Art School and by 1909 was studying at the Boston Museum of Fine Arts School. As a student he was already firm in his love for painting in nature. Despite finding studio painting constricting and claustrophobic, Hibbard's remarkable skill as a figure painter was confirmed by his teacher Joseph DeCamp who chastised him for making figure painting look too easy.

Winning a coveted scholarship to travel to Europe, Hibbard left in 1913. More intrigued by

Carlson's Quarry, Rockport
1920 OIL ON CANVAS 28" X 33"
COLLECTION OF ROCKPORT NATIONAL BANK
see. 94

(OPPOSITE)
Winter, Rockport Harbor
CA. 1940 OIL ON CANVAS 17" X 20"
PRIVATE COLLECTION
PHOTO COURTESY OF VOSE GALLERIES OF BOSTON

Impressionism than by the other burgeoning modernist styles, Hibbard pursued the technique while traveling through England, France, Spain, Morocco and Italy. In Spain he was greatly impressed when he met Joaquin Sorolla in his studio. He knew he had met a man of like-minded philosophy when Sorolla told him that the studio "was a good place to smoke."[29]

Hibbard's sojourn in Europe was cut short by the First World War. After returning to America in 1914, he eventually settled in Provincetown, taking winter excursions to Vermont. Very pleased with the picturesque streets of Provincetown, Hibbard initially turned down his friend Charles Knapp's request that he come inspect Cape Ann for himself. After a visit in 1919, Hibbard moved to Rockport the following year, renting Tucker Margeson's old studio on Atlantic Avenue. His first year there he began the Rockport Summer School of Painting. In 1921, the famous meeting that brought the formation of the Rockport Art Association was held at his studio. He was elected the first secretary. Hibbard joined the town's baseball team as a player and eventually a manager. During the Second World War, he raffled off his paintings to pay for team equipment, just as he had done years earlier to support the baseball team he founded in art school.

Hibbard maintained his tradition of going to Vermont during the winter to paint snow draped landscapes. But necessity brought new innovation to his style. Broken color application may work for summer painters, but frost bite, frozen paints and winter gales that blow away canvases forced Hibbard to find quicker ways to capture the light and atmosphere of winter. He began to apply paint more broadly to cover the canvas quickly, as he once said, "You're up against time to get it all down. I had to find a manner to capture it in the weather conditions I worked in."[30] Tromping through the countryside, snow shoes on, lugging fifty pounds of painting equipment at the first light of dawn, Hibbard became a master of his elements, creating a vast body of work in conditions few other artists could withstand. As an early observer of Hibbard's work wrote, "It is a far cry from Bohemianism."[31]

Ann Fisk, the former Director of the Rockport Art Association said in an interview, "The idea of painting in lovely weather and apple orchards has been with us a long time, but the idea that, in winter, one could get out there, showed it could be done and not from photographs. There's no substitute for feeling the cold, it shows in his work."[32]

Hibbard sought the same invigoration in painting as he did in baseball. He used to tell students, "Paint with speed. Use up your nervous energy. A morning's painting should wear you out."[33] Hibbard maintained his school for 30 years. He was a gifted teacher who inspired his students with few words, and despite his more traditional values, he never frowned upon any style or approach. He juried shows, ran exhibitions, held fund raisers and was responsible for producing the proper mixture of red paint whenever the town icon, Motif #1, needed a fresh coat. He often spoke on behalf of the town to preserve the traditional, quaint appearance of Rockport. He once told the Rockport Town Fathers, "The town's alright; leave it alone."[34]

see page 5

Winter Motif #1
CA. 1930 OIL ON CANVAS 25" X 30"
PRIVATE COLLECTION
PHOTO COURTESY OF VOSE GALLERIES

WILLIAM MEYEROWITZ

1887 – 1981

BORN IN EKSTERINOSLAV in the Ukraine, William and his father fled political turbulence and came to New York in 1908. Meyerowitz was raised with art; his father, a singer, had encouraged both art and music. It is said that by the age of eight young William was drawing Russian market scenes. These two passions would sustain him throughout his life. By 1912 Meyerowitz was training at the National Academy of Design while supporting himself as a choral singer for the Metropolitan Opera.

Meyerowitz was a part of the group of New York painters with Robert Henri and George Bellows that founded the People's Art Guild in hopes of creating interest in art outside the main-

stream New York galleries. In 1919, Meyerowitz married Theresa Bernstein, also a painter in New York. Bernstein introduced Meyerowitz to Cape Ann. When the two first traveled to the region, they stayed on Eastern Point in Gloucester in the same home later occupied by Marsden Hartley. It became a lifelong tradition, winters in New York and summers on Cape Ann.

Gloucester's West End is a classic example of Meyerowitz' skills and fascination with outdoor activity. A series of oil washes gives the picture the appearance of a watercolor, lending a lightness not often found in oil. Showing the view of the Italian end of Main street with City Hall in the background, the image captures both activity

Still Life with Open Window
1925 OIL ON CANVAS 30" X 36"
PRIVATE COLLECTION

(OPPOSITE)
Gloucester's West End
CA. LATE 1920'S OIL ON CANVAS 25" X 30"
PRIVATE COLLECTION

and serenity in its rendering of specific detail with very loose brushwork. Rather than avoiding evidence of the modern era, like so many artists of the period, Meyerowitz chose to include automobiles. This was characteristic of the Ash Can circle of painters who strove to paint modern life and its industrial changes with truth. Meyerowitz' *Still Life with Open Window*, painted in 1925, shows a different side of the artist's range. Reminiscent of Cezanne, the image combines both the loose brushwork and spontaneity of his street scenes with the more academic, detailed rendering of the embroidered table cloth.

Meyerowitz was very active in the area, submitting his work to numerous exhibitions. He was also an etcher and is credited with several innovations in the medium of color etching. In the 1920's both Meyerowitz and Bernstein often visited Ellen Day Hale at her home in Folly Cove, staying in a cottage provided by Hale called "Gaviota." Meyerowitz eventually bought a house on Mount Pleasant Street in East Gloucester which became his home, studio and the classroom for the courses he taught in the summer months.

MARTHA WALTER

1875 – 1976

BORN IN PHILADELPHIA, Martha Walter had shown exceptional skill in drawing and painting so young that by the time she was in high school she was already studying with William Merritt Chase at the Pennsylvania Academy of Fine Arts. Something of a prodigy, she was excused from much of the rudimentary drawing courses and was allowed to pursue oil painting directly. Encouraged to compete for awards and prizes, Walter won a scholarship to study in Europe in 1908. Her two year stay stretched to several more as she traveled and studied in Holland, France, Spain and Italy. Attending the Grand-Chaumiére and later the Académie Julian, Walter became frustrated with the claustrophobia of studio work. She discovered her passion for plein air painting along the Atlantic coast, working in Biarritz, Dinard, St. Malo and Trouville. She might have become a permanent expatriate had it not been for the First World War.

Back in New England, Walter's love for painting sun-filled, outdoor gatherings compelled her to search for similar locales in America. This led her to Coney Island then to Cape Ann. For the next several years she spent her summers in Gloucester and started her first class as a teacher. Walter had an attraction to beach life like Edward Potthast and with both oils and watercolors she captured the light and harmony of color with movement in pictures like *Good Harbor Beach*. In contrast to her summer vacation pictures is *In Port, Gloucester*, showing a group of fishermen mending nets on deck. Despite its loose rendering, details like handle-bar mustaches, tobacco pipes and faces deeply tanned from hours on the ocean make the image a wonderful cultural document of Cape Ann's history. Walter's love for painting families and especially children on the shore helped to shape and popularize the fame of the Cape as a vacation spot.

Good Harbor Beach
CA. 1930 OIL ON CANVAS 16" X 20"
PRIVATE COLLECTION
PHOTO COURTESY OF
GREENWICH GALLERY

In Port, Gloucester
CA. LATE 1920'S OIL ON CANVAS 21" X 36"
PRIVATE COLLECTION
PHOTO COURTESY OF VOSE GALLERIES

HUGH BRECKENRIDGE

1870 - 1937

"GLOUCESTER HAS everything the artist wants, except mountains,"[35] Breckenridge once said in an interview in 1926. By then he had already established himself as an exceptional teacher and also as a painter perpetually redefining his art. Ever since staring at a reproduction of Raphael's *Madonna of the Chair* as a young child, Breckenridge became thoroughly devoted to art. Studies in school were replaced by endless sketching and doodling. That which created trouble in grade school brought him great success at the Pennsylvania Academy of Fine Arts which he began attending in 1887. Scholarships later led to study in Paris at the Académie Julian and with William Adolphe Bouguereau. Breckenridge's exposure to an academic teacher like Bouguereau made a strong impact on his skills, later revealed in his portraiture. However, it was French Impressionism that contributed most to Breckenridge's quest: innovation and experimentation.

The fin-de-siècle era was a time of incredible diversity of styles, theories and experimentation in the art world, and Breckenridge was open to them all. His attraction to Impressionism was strong and he excelled in the broken, vivid color techniques of the French, but he did not stop there. The next several decades of his life were an endless exploration of Post-Impressionism, Fauvism, Abstraction, Cubism and Modernism. Observing a body of his work, one can find Sargent-esque portraits of high society women, fauvist still-lifes and abstract, non-representational scenes overlapping and reoccurring throughout his career.

Breckenridge devoted great energy to teaching, including running a summer school with

Building, Gloucester
CA. 1920 OIL ON BOARD 15" X 15"
PRIVATE COLLECTION
PHOTO COURTESY OF DAVID HALL
FINE WORKS OF ART & APPRAISALS

(OPPOSITE)
Old City Hall, Gloucester
1930 OIL ON CANVAS 25" X 30"
PRIVATE COLLECTION
PHOTO COURTESY OF MCCLEES GALLERIES

Thomas Anshutz. When he arrived on Cape Ann in 1920, he opened the Breckenridge School of Artists in East Gloucester. He loved the harbors and explored wide ranges of color and paint application, but his work began to return towards the initial Impressionistic style that first attracted him to modernism. Many of his Cape Ann scenes are somewhat Fauvist with hot, intense color. Others like, *Old City Hall, Gloucester* recall more the influences of Monet and even Van Gogh. Broken bursts of color replace form, but there are also the swirling brush strokes of the Van Gogh style that had so awed Brecken-

ridge when he traveled to Holland. Having arrived on Cape Ann at the relatively mature age of 50, Breckenridge nevertheless allowed it to affect his art like an open-minded student. Never one to grow complacent in his style, he continued to experiment into his last years, thus as a teacher passing on the principles of impressionism to students for which Cape Ann is so well known, but also advocating the many avenues of Modernism.

Breckenridge was a member of the North Shore Arts Association and maintained his school in East Gloucester for seventeen years until his death.

HARRIET RANDALL LUMIS
1870 – 1953

BY THE TIME Lumis visited Cape Ann for the first time to study with Hugh Breckenridge she was already fifty and had long established herself as a serious artist. Born and raised in Salem, Connecticut, near Old Lyme, Lumis overcame the limited encouragement usually given to women in the Victorian age and pursued her interest in art. Married young, her husband, an architect was fortunately enthusiastic about her aspirations. She pursued them with zeal. Early studies with Willie S. Adams had given her work a Tonalist quality. Given her proximity to the Old Lyme painters and the general trends of the time, Lumis' work evolved to Impressionism. By 1910, she was studying under Leonard Ochtman and shortly thereafter began to exhibit her work.

Lumis had a natural gift for Impressionism. Her eye for color and light was sophisticated and well developed, all the more surprising for she never set foot in Europe. In 1920 Lumis took her first trip to East Gloucester to seek out Hugh Breckenridge's school on Rocky Neck. Lumis was clearly Breckenridge's oldest student, but her desire to learn and refine her technique continued throughout her career. Her pictures of Gloucester and Rockport have an earthy gusto with strong color and light, somewhat reminiscent of Kuehne's work. Her painting of *Five Pound Island* is topographically of interest since it no longer exists—landfill now connects the island to the mainland.

Lumis is unique in American art of that era; historians recall her as being one of the only woman painters of pure landscape subjects who never adopted the Post-Impressionistic trends that developed in America in the early twentieth century. The pre-Depression years saw the height of Lumis' financial and critical success. During the Depression her career suffered and she taught to supplement her income. She never regained the stature she had previously achieved, and the death of her husband in 1937 along with the changes in the art world had separated her from popular trends. She continued to paint until the end of her life, however, and she always sought through organizations to encourage traditional realist and academic painting.

Evening at Gloucester
CA. 1925 OIL ON BOARD 12" X 10"
PRIVATE COLLECTION
PHOTO COURTESY OF DAVIES FINE ARTS

Five Pound Island
CA. 1925 OIL ON CANVAS 24" X 28"
PRIVATE COLLECTION
PHOTO COURTESY OF R.H. LOVE GALLERIES

MARSDEN HARTLEY

1877 - 1943

ACKNOWLEDGED today as a pioneer of modern art in America, Hartley's life was a series of restless flights from country to country as he strove for artistic inspiration, emotional well-being and an ever-elusive inner peace. Hartley's visits to Cape Ann brought a brief respite to this turmoil, and he found it in the most unlikely place.

As a young artist in New York Hartley became friends with Alfred Stieglitz, whose "291" Gallery held his first one man show in 1909. It was Stieglitz who helped him make his first trip to Europe in 1912. Hartley worked in France and Germany, submerged in the modernist scene and its various styles. He had phases of Expressionism and Cubism, some imitations of European modernists, others of great originality. After returning to America in 1918, Hartley made his first trip to Cape Ann in 1920, staying at 1 Eastern Point Road in East Gloucester. Much of what is known of Hartley's experience on Cape Ann comes from letters he wrote to Steiglitz. Hartley also wrote prose and poetry and had found a renewed ener-

gy for both in Gloucester. He wrote Steiglitz from Gloucester that he "worked hard for the past 8 weeks, painting and writing every day to keep the wolf of mediocrity from gnawing at the aristocratic vitals of true ambition."[36] Occasionally in the company of Stuart Davis and Theresa Bernstein, he avoided art circles and never exhibited in the region. It was on this trip that he also discovered Dogtown.

Despite Cape Ann's rejuvenating quality, Hartley left the United States again and remained overseas for the next ten years. The twenties saw great innovation and experimentation in Hartley's work. He abandoned Expressionism and pursued landscape painting. Often described in biographies, his constant travels also point to a deep restlessness, indicative of a tortured soul. By the time Hartley returned to America, he was emotionally and physically exhausted. His art was suffering, and after a dreadful winter in New York, he returned to the coastal town that he remembered so fondly.

Rock Doxology, Dogtown
1931 OIL ON PANEL 18" X 24"
PRIVATE COLLECTION

(OPPOSITE)
Summer Outward Bound, Dogtown
1931 OIL ON PANEL 18 1/4" X 24"
PRIVATE COLLECTION

Arriving in 1931, Hartley moved into the same residence he previously occupied. Eager to return to Dogtown, Hartley was soon wandering the mysterious inland hills that had captured his imagination ten years before. He reflected later:

"I wanted to go back to New England again - I had seen some rocks twelve [sic] years before that when I was in Gloucester and Gloucester is one of those you want to go back to—I had remembered the rocks and the name Dogtown—that's a great name—and no one in all the years of Gloucester painting had ever done anything about Dogtown..."[37]

Hartley began painting the colossal boulder and rock formations amidst the terminal glacier moraine. He also wrote several poems about Gloucester and Dogtown. The area brought a deep peace to Hartley who likened it to a church, the closest to a religious experience he'd ever known. The mixture of stones, open sky and ruins of early settlements brought Hartley a tranquility he'd rarely felt. Wandering alone amidst the rocks, he felt himself in an otherwordly sanctuary, writing that Dogtown "looks like a cross between Easter Island and Stonehenge, essentially Druidic in appearance."[38]

A true Steppenwolf, Hartley often felt a great distance from other artists, especially the more traditional painters who came to Cape Ann to join in the legacy of harbor painting. But he once confessed to Steiglitz in a letter that he hoped to be remembered as the painter of Dogtown.

"Dogtown," he said, "is mine."[39]

MILTON AVERY

1885 – 1965

POVERTY AND deaths in the family were not enough to prevent Avery from pursuing art. By the time he was a young man, Avery's father and both of his brothers had died. As the sole bread-winner for an extended family of women, he worked for years in factory jobs. However, enough encouragement in a single art instruction class led him to devote himself to a career. An art class under Charles Noel Flagg at the Connectictut League of Art Students deeply affected him and influenced his techniques in the many years to come. Avery's signature style did not fully develop until he was almost in his sixties. Like many other artists during the dawn of modernism, several years of his career were spent

shedding the traditional influence and techniques of the time. When he came to Gloucester for the first time in 1920, Avery's work was strongly influenced by Ernest Lawson, John H. Twachtman and other American Impressionists.

The light and atmosphere of Cape Ann, however, made Avery develop new techniques. Like Stuart Davis, with subsequent visits each summer, Avery began painting from sketches rather than from nature. He moved away from thicker brush work which he felt distracted people from the purpose of the picture, preoccupying them with the way it was painted, not the painting itself. Therefore, he began using the palette knife less and painted in broader strokes, applying the

Bridge to the Sea
1937 GOUACHE 23 1/4" X 17"
COLLECTION OF THE CAPE ANN
HISTORICAL ASSOCIATION

The Nancy B.
1944 GOUACHE 21 1/4" X 30"
COLLECTION OF THE CAPE ANN
HISTORICAL ASSOCIATION

paint thinly. He became more interested in light and how it played with colors. During his fourth summer on Cape Ann in 1924, Avery met Sally Michel in Gloucester; two years later they were married and honeymooned on Cape Ann. The Great Depression did not prevent Avery from pursuing his passion; if anything it only made local room and board on Cape Ann more affordable. In 1932, Avery's daughter March was born. Over the next several years, he would depict her in paintings numerous times. Watercolor and gouache figured more prominently in his work as well. Having abandoned plein air painting for sketch work on paper, he was freed of having to lug around his pictures, and he began using larger canvases.

For several visits Avery and his wife stayed at the Mother Ann Cottage on Eastern Point near the Lighthouse. Among the Cape Ann painters in residence at the time, Avery was sometimes in the company of artists like Marsden Hartley and William Meyerowitz. He tended to remain outside of the larger circles of painters, though he did exhibit locally at the Gloucester Society of Artists. Avery's last visits came in the summers from 1943 to 1945. By then he was receiving more critical attention and deliberately sought out the quiet of Cape Ann as a counter balance. He is now regarded as one of the most important colorists of the twentieth century who, by the 1960's, had greatly influenced modern American art.

FELICIE WALDO HOWELL

1897 - 1968

HOWELL WAS exposed to New England and the harbors of Cape Ann from the deck of her husband's yacht. Born in Honolulu, she moved to Washington D.C. by 1917 where she began training at the Corcoran Art School with Edmund Messer. Later she moved to Pennsylvania where she studied at the Philadelphia School of Design for Women with Henry B. Snell, a New Hope Impressionist. Her earliest years as an artist were spent painting mostly interior scenes. When she married George Mixter, he was already an accomplished yachtsman, and the two took boating trips along the east coast aboard his schooner Teragram. Many of her watercolors were painted aboard the vessel during their frequent visits to each harbor. One of the highlights of her career was a series of pictures of the America's Cup Races in 1937. She eventually became a respected teacher at the New York School of Applied Art and Painting.

Howell made frequent painting trips to Cape Ann harbors, always leaving again on her husband's boat. Between 1947 and 1953 however, she did establish residence in Rockport. Painted in 1923, *Gloucester Wharf* is an exceptional example of her startling dexterity with watercolor. Stripped of color, save for the sharp green of the boat's hull, the picture is almost monochromatic. Mixing both broad wet washes and tight, concise brushwork, it bears the influence of Maurice Prendergast and Jane Peterson, especially in the chaotic lines and squiggles in the water. With so limited a palette, that Howell is still able to deliver such contrast and bold color is remarkable. She presents a view of a harbor celebrated for its vast range of bright and intense color and creates an image made up of textures of brown and tan, decontextualizing a familiar place until it appears entirely foreign.

Howell exhibited her work in many shows and often received great praise for her work in art catalogues and periodicals of the time, but posthumous scholarly research has not yet been forthcoming. With time, hopefully her work will be properly catalogued and fully appreciated.

Gloucester Wharf
1923 WATERCOLOR 19 1/2" X 26"
PRIVATE COLLECTION
PHOTO COURTESY OF DAVIES FINE ARTS

ANTONIO CIRINO

1889 – 1983

BORN IN SERINO, ITALY, Antonio came to America at the age of two, settling in Providence, Rhode Island in a neighborhood of Italian immigrants. He developed a passion for visual art from cutting out illustrations from popular magazines of the day. As his collection grew so did his intentions for the future. Before his arrival on Cape Ann, Antonio Cirino had studied at the Rhode Island School of Design and returned there as a teacher after receiving a Bachelor's Degree from Columbia University in 1912. With the outbreak of the First World War, Cirino served with the State Department deciphering enemy coded messages and returned to Europe as a member of the American Staff at the Versailles Peace Treaty. Despite the war, his growing love of art, writing and jewelry making never wavered.

Cirino's first trip to Rockport came in the summer of 1921 where he shared a studio with Parker Perkins. Later he bought a home in Pigeon Cove and began a tradition of teaching in the academic year at the Rhode Island School of Design and summering on Cape Ann. He also co-wrote a book, *Jewelry Making and Design* and penned two books, *The Etruscans and Their Jewelry Making* and *The Arnold Silver*. He also had periods as a teacher at schools in Indiana and Illinois. But these endeavors never hampered his painting; they are merely evidence of a multi-faceted, learned man. He pursued his paintings of the

Spring Touch Up
1952 OIL ON BOARD 8" X 10"
PRIVATE COLLECTION

(OPPOSITE)
Pigeon Cove
CA. 1950 OIL ON BOARD 8" X 10"
PRIVATE COLLECTION
PHOTO COURTESY OF DAVIES FINE ARTS

region with great energy, creating warm, impressionistic images of the houses, harbors and streets.

He was a founding member of the Rockport Art Association and became one of its first directors. Over his life he won seventy five awards and held numerous exhibitions locally and nationally. Cirino's passion for teaching was strong and he brought a writer's eloquence to the task with words of wisdom which he often wrote down for students to read. Excerpts like, "There is plenty of luck in hard work. Grow by embracing its acrostic: Go Right On Working," and "Work in the spirit of Michelangelo: he burned barrels of sketches to conceal his hard work,"[40] are wonderful examples of his desire to create awareness and attention in young students. Near the end of his life, at the age of 89, when hearing a younger man's surprise that a man of his age was still painting, Cirino replied, "I don't still paint, I *vigorously* paint!"[41]

CLAIRE SHUTTLEWORTH

1868 – 1930

TODAY SHUTTLEWORTH is well remembered for her many paintings of Niagara Falls and the surrounding region. Born and raised in Buffalo, she was most associated with the city throughout her life, becoming the prominent woman painter of the region. She studied at the Art Student's League with George Bridgman, trained in Europe with Luc-Olivier Merson in Paris and traveled with Frank Vincent DuMond in France and Italy. Graduating from the École des Beaux-Arts in 1897, Shuttleworth eventually returned to America, and by the early 1910's had established a studio in Ontario. Her work of this period explored the many moods and facets of Niagara Falls; today this body of work is considered among the finest of all Niagara paintings.

Shuttleworth became a member of the Rockport Art Association in 1923, though exactly when she made her first visit to Cape Ann is unclear. Some writers of Shuttleworth's career describe a recurring theme in her work of natural environments blending or clashing with evidence of the industrial era. Later her work evolved to include more pictures throughout New England as well as an exploration of floral still-lifes. Painted in the 1920's *Inner Harbor* is a great example of Shuttleworth's strong academic training under artists like DuMond. It is also a unique image of Cape Ann by an early woman painter outside of the influence of either Jane Peterson or the Boston style of the Hales. The color palette is somewhat darker than many of the Impressionist pictures of the time, perhaps revealing the influence of earlier European styles of the previous century.

Newspaper clippings from the 1920's document shows in which Shuttleworth won first prize over other artists such as Charles Burchfield and Carl W. Peters. Her death at 62 ended a career that had only grown in prestige.

Inner Harbor
CA. 1923 OIL ON CANVAS 20" X 24"
PRIVATE COLLECTION
PHOTO COURTESY OF DAVIES FINE ARTS

CARL W. PETERS
1897 – 1980

REMEMBERED BY friends and artists as kind, humble, encouraging and non-competitive, Peters was first and foremost singularly obsessed with painting. He also spent more summers on Cape Ann than most other artists of any era—close to sixty summers. In that time, he occasionally taught classes, exhibited often and befriended many artists and locals. Like fellow artist William Lester Stevens, the business of art interested him little; he shied from praise and was often pained to see his pictures leave his possession. He lived only for the physical process of painting.

Born in Rochester, New York, Peters spent his student days at the Rochester Mechanics Institute before World War I took him to France where he served as a camouflage artist. Back in America, he studied at the Art Student's League, training under Charles Rosen and Harry Leith-Ross and later under John F. Carlson during summers in Woodstock. While still in his early twenties, Peters established a pattern in his life that he maintained almost unchanged for the next six decades: winters in Fairport, summers in Rockport. He befriended both Charles and Emile Gruppe, teaching together with Emile in the summer of 1931, maintaining a lifelong friendship.

Peters' single minded pursuit of plein air painting had over the years produced a large body of pictures of boats, harbors, shipyards, street scenes and landscapes that blend Impressionism, Post-Impressionism and elements of Fauvism and Modernism. He later became associated with the "Rationalists," a group of painters of the Genesee region of New York where he lived, that believed art should be an evolution, not a revolution. There was little motivation in him to make money or enhance his reputation in wider circles. Even as a teacher he appeared only to want to encourage students rather than create groups of followers. For him there was only the process of painting. The rest, it seems, was merely window dressing.

Winter Days, Gloucester
CA. 1950 OIL ON CANVAS 20" X 24"
PRIVATE COLLECTION
PHOTO COURTESY OF DAVIES FINE ARTS

GIFFORD BEAL

1879 — 1956

SEVERAL YEARS younger than his brother and fellow artist, Reynolds, Gifford Beal showed a very early interest in art yet chose to pursue a different path. Most significantly, he never studied nor cared to study in Europe. Other than a brief trip after college graduation and a honeymoon visit, Beal never set foot in Europe again, and even actively avoided Paris while there. What may at first appear to be a narrow minded attitude only hints at the uniqueness of his character.

By the early age of thirteen Gifford was training under William Merritt Chase, accompanying Reynolds, then 25, to the Shinnecock School on Long Island. Often described as very business like, Gifford Beal was renowned for the conservative, orderly structuring of his life. This may have been born of his wealthy upbringing in New York City. This environment may have also shaped the subject matter that he chose to paint, often leisurely scenes in Central Park. Beal became intrigued with painting festivals, circuses and parades, any place of frenetic, human activity. He sought to capture movement and action, the dynamic nature of the immediate. These inclinations made Cape Ann a natural destination during an era when the fishing industry, quarry digging and the dawn of tourism were melding into one another.

It is believed that Beal first came to Rockport in 1922, and he was immediately enamored with the possibilities for painting. Gifford was in love with the sea his whole career and took several trips all over the Caribbean. The light and colors of the coast intrigued him, but Rockport was forever his home away from New York. Beal's diversity of style is remarkable. Capable of rendering impressionistic harbor scenes, Beal could also create icon-like images such as *Sea Bass Fisherman*, reminiscent of N.C. Wyeth and The Brandywine Tradition.

Beal established a studio in a refurbished home on Atlantic Avenue overlooking Sandy Bay and the harbor. His enthusiasm about Rockport was strong enough that he encouraged his brother Reynolds and other friends like George Bellows, and quite remarkably, General George S. Patton to visit the area. Gifford was known to have visited most of the art colonies throughout New England but was only truly pleased with the robust, raw nature of Cape Ann. In his youth, Beal sat among future greats Edward Hopper, Georgia O'Keefe and George Bellows. This and the total absence of European influence in his training may have made Gifford Beal a purely American Painter.

Rockport Inner Harbor
CA. 1930 OIL ON CANVAS 30" X 24"
PRIVATE COLLECTION

Sea Bass Fisherman
CA. 1940 OIL ON BOARD 20" X 24"
COLLECTION OF THE WESTMORELAND MUSEUM OF AMERICAN ART,
221 NORTH MAIN STREET, GREENSBURG, PA 15601-1898
ANONYMOUS GIFT THROUGH THE WESTMORELAND SOCIETY, 1995

REYNOLDS BEAL

1867 - 1951

THOUGH SEVERAL years younger, it was his brother Gifford who motivated Reynolds Beal to become more serious about the artistic interests he had pursued since the age of seven. After Reynolds' period of study in Madrid, in 1890 both brothers attended William Merritt Chase's Shinnecock School on Long Island, perhaps the first plein air painting school in America. Reynolds decided to pursue art for life after abandoning a potential career in naval architecture. All the Beal children, one daughter and four brothers, had been raised with boating and sailing, and these outdoor activities were to set the course for Reynolds' life. Resisting family pressure for a formal career, he dropped out of Cornell University to pursue art. Reynolds was fortunate to live off a family stipend which freed him from the toils of earning a living. This freedom enabled a life of extravagant adventures and painting trips. Unlike his brother who remained for most of his life in America, Reynolds traveled to every corner of the globe including the Middle East, Africa, the Far East, South East Asia, Australia and South America, sometimes at the helm of his own sailing yacht.

Reynolds found his way to Cape Ann after a long association with the Provincetown community of painters. After continuous persistence from his brother, Reynolds joined him in Rockport in 1922. Eventually he and his wife moved into their own studio on Atlantic Avenue and Reynolds quickly went to work creating a great number of bright impressionist pictures as well as many etchings of the coastal life of the Cape.

Rockport Harbor
1922 OIL ON CANVAS 24" X 40"
PRIVATE COLLECTION
PHOTO COURTESY OF
VOSE GALLERIES OF BOSTON

Wallace Brothers' Circus, Gloucester
1941 OIL ON MASONITE 12" X 16"
COLLECTION OF ALLEN NAHMAN
PHOTO COURTESY OF ROYAL GALLERIES

Despite the differences in their future careers and lives, both Reynolds and Gifford had very similar tastes in their choice of subject matter. Reynolds loved the outdoors and all the frenzy of human activity that could be found in the country, in parks, harbors, shipyards and all summertime places of leisure, especially circuses. Though he abandoned a naval career, Reynolds remained in love with the sea and with boating. Over the years he painted every conceivable kind of sea vessel in every kind of weather.

Beal was always open to the influences of other artistic styles burgeoning in Europe and America,

and by the time he painted *Wallace Brothers' Circus, Gloucester* his style was very affected by Van Gogh. Beal spent the last twenty years of his life living in the area. He traveled the globe, painting in many exotic locales but always returned to Cape Ann. Because of his financial freedom, Reynolds was never under the pressure to exhibit as often as his brother Gifford who for mysterious reasons never benefited from his father's benevolence. Consequently Reynolds' work is less publicized and records are fewer charting the course of his career. Towards the end of his life, illness limited his energies and his output.

SAMUEL F. HERSHEY

1904 - 1987

MOST FONDLY remembered as a teacher, Samuel F. Hershey had some of the best teachers in the region. After he attended the Massachusetts Institute of Technology and the Pennsylvania Academy of Fine Arts, a chance visit to Rockport in 1923 brought Hershey back again and again where he spent periods studying under Aldro T. Hibbard and later William Lester Stevens.

While still a student under these masters, Hershey began to teach both at the Cambridge School of Architecture and at Harvard University. He accompanied Stevens to Europe in the 1930's as his assistant. Hershey made good use of the WPA era, painting murals in public buildings in Rockport and beyond. *New England Coast* is a great example of Hibbard's influence on Hershey. Painted outdoors, the picture shows Hershey's tendency towards a more exaggerated composition and increased angularity in the structures than found in Hibbard's or Stevens' work. This gives Hershey a slightly more modern feel than his two esteemed teachers. The combination of desolation created through the absence of people with the warmth of late afternoon light casting complex shadows creates a guarded but palpable sense of invitation; it is not a foreboding feeling.

A portrait of his wife, *Ellie* clearly shows his skills in rendering the figure. It seems to call back to Italian Renaissance portraiture in which a detailed backdrop is clearly visible yet separated from the figure in a curious, dreamlike fashion. The woman is given an almost divine quality as she stands illuminated in a halo. The picture blends a traditional portraiture approach with more innovative brushwork and color mixture. The use of Motif #1 makes the location undeniable, yet the high elevation of the woman and the topography of the landscape are inventions by the artist. The outcome is a highly original blend of a landscape, a harbor scene, and a portrait with allegorical overtones.

Hershey served as an officer in the Army Air Corps during the Second World War. After the war he became a teacher at the Rhode Island School of Design, but always returned to Rockport. In 1947 Hershey took over the position of president for the Rockport Art Association which he occupied for four years.

Ellie
1930 OIL ON CANVAS 47 1/2" X 39 1/2"
COLLECTION OF THE CAPE ANN
HISTORICAL ASSOCIATION

New England Coast
CA. MID 1930'S OIL ON CANVAS 30" X 36"
COLLECTION OF THE TOWN OF ROCKPORT

MARGUERITE S. PEARSON

1898 - 1978

THE STORY OF Marguerite Pearson has tragic beginnings, but her life became a triumph of courage and spirit. Born in Philadelphia and raised in Somerville, Massachusetts, Marguerite enjoyed a normal childhood until the age of sixteen when she was stricken with polio. It was during her long convalescence that she began to draw and paint in order to occupy her time and distract her thoughts. From this terrible, debilitating illness that left her a paraplegic came the seeds of the path for her to follow that bore much fruit.

Bound to a wheelchair she began taking courses at the Boston Museum School, where her determination and drive kept her intensely active; she also had the good fortune of studying under many of the best painters in Boston. Early classes were taken with Chase Emerson and Harold Anderson. Later she studied figure painting with William James, anatomy classes with Frederick Bosley, and still later she came under the training of Philip Leslie Hale and Aldro T. Hibbard. Eventually she followed extended studies with Edmund C. Tarbell who greatly influenced her.

Pearson's first priority seems to have been to support herself. Despite her disabilities she was determined to be independent, to not be a hindrance to her family. Living in the Fenway studios in Boston she began work as an illustrator as she continued classes in the Boston Museum School. By the early twenties she had made the switch to being a professional painter and had her first one-woman show in 1924 which was received with great critical praise. The art critic A.J. Philpot of the Boston Globe stated, "....these are the works of a rare genius—of one who already ranks high and is destined to achieve unusual distinction in the art world."[42] It was around this time that she began spending her summers in Rockport.

Despite the difficulties Pearson had in moving about outdoors she still produced some admirable harbor pictures, often viewed from her back porch overlooking the water. What she did excel at and became most noted for were her indoor pictures usually of women in long dresses, often playing a musical instrument, drawing or reading. They have a grandness that recalls the regal Victorian era and also have a similar quality to William Paxton's interior scenes of women. Pearson was a very social person and became involved in many artists' circles on Cape Ann even before moving there full time in 1942. From then on she was very active in the Rockport Art Association. She became a sought after teacher and often worked as a juror at shows. She spent the next thirty years living in Rockport.

Pearson is a symbol of the triumph of pure will over one's physical debilitations. Rather than becoming a painter merely for therapy, she excelled in the fine arts, winning many awards and finally becoming a gifted teacher, never giving in to self-pity. Truly she was a painter who happened to be a paraplegic, not the other way around.

The Wedding March
CA. 1940 OIL ON CANVAS 36" X 40"
COLLECTION OF THE SEAWARD INN

MARGUERITE S. PEARSON

The Visit
CA. 1940 OIL ON CANVAS 36" X 30"
PRIVATE COLLECTION
PHOTO COURTESY OF VOSE GALLERIES OF BOSTON

MAURICE COMPRIS

1885 – 1939

BORN IN AMSTERDAM, Compris had all his early training in his native Holland, studying at the Quellinus School and at the Royal Academy in Amsterdam. He painted and traveled in England before coming to the United States in his early twenties. Settling in New York, Compris became a furniture designer as well as a painter of murals, portraits and still life subjects. Over his life he established his reputation with several major commissions for murals in churches, public buildings and theaters. When Compris first came to Cape Ann is unclear, but by 1924 he had become a member of the Rockport Art Association.

Compris and his wife Frieda often held court with friends Aldro T. Hibbard, William Lester Stevens and Emile and Charles Gruppe in their studio at 2 Mill Lane. With his European training, Compris became an adept, sought after portrait painter on Cape Ann, producing excellent pictures of friends, fellow artists and sitters. Though a resident of Rockport, Compris maintained a studio in Boston throughout his life.

Compris' *Portrait of Sam Hershey* is an excellent example of his ability to capture the personality and character of a sitter. Compris and Hershey were good friends which seems quite apparent in the painting; Compris has rendered a likeness of Hershey which is intimate and personable, revealing the comfort of both the sitter and the artist. This was also a requirement for Compris, that he be comfortable with the nature of a commission and his ability to carry it out in the manner he desired. A portrait painter for high society in New York and Boston as well, he was known to refuse portrait commissions if the nature of the work and the circumstances for painting were not to his liking.

Students remembered Compris as an excellent teacher, though "rather gruff."[43] He is also remembered as highly compassionate towards animals, easily brought to tears at their suffering. He had a particular enthusiasm for the Rockport Art Association's costume balls, organizing and insisting on masks and costumes for all members. Some of his murals can still be found in Massachusetts. Most significantly he did the ceiling decoration in Our Lady of Good Voyage Church in Gloucester. When Compris died of cancer in 1939 he was the acting Vice President for the Rockport Art Association.

Portrait of Sam Hershey
1937 OIL ON CANVAS 44" X 36"
COLLECTION OF THE CAPE ANN
HISTORICAL ASSOCIATION

CHARLES GRUPPE

1860 – 1940

WHEN CHARLES Gruppe arrived in Rockport with his son Emile, he had long established himself as a fine landscape painter in Europe. Though born in Canada, Gruppe had ventured to Europe and submerged himself in artistic circles in Holland and spent over twenty years studying, painting and thriving among European dealers and buyers. Gruppe had become such a master of the Dutch School and its techniques that he often managed to surpass native Dutchmen for highly coveted positions such as in the Pulchre Studio. His pictures had even been purchased by Queen Emma and Queen Wilhelmina.

The outbreak of the First World War forced Gruppe to relocate the family to the United States. Charles Gruppe spent several more years as a painter in New York before he and Emile came to Cape Ann together for the first time in 1925. Settling in Rockport, they moved into Blanche Brink's Crow's Nest on Bearskin Neck. With his pictures in the private collections of European royalty and his new fame in the New York and Rochester art circles well established, the elder Gruppe's international reputation added further prestige to the region. Among the many young painters of Cape Ann was now a European master. Gruppe's darker, tonal style of the Dutch School began to exhibit a more colorful palette, a lighter tone and influences of Impressionism.

Despite the great artists that had already spent time on Cape Ann, the number of available venues for painters to locally display their works was

The Granite Pier
CA. 1930 OIL ON PANEL 12" X 16"
COLLECTION OF SANDY BAY HISTORICAL
SOCIETY AND MUSEUMS

(OPPOSITE)

Rockport Harbor and the Motif   *see page 5*
CA. 1935 OIL ON PANEL 12" X 16"
PRIVATE COLLECTION
PHOTO COURTESY OF THE COOLEY GALLERY

still limited. For the lack of better facilities, Charles Gruppe was not above displaying his and Emile's pictures at a local coffee shop. Though having to resort to such means vexed many local artists at times, including Gruppe, such a story is symbolic of the raw freshness of the region at a time when institutions were few and the paths were not yet beaten.

Like Duveneck, Gruppe's respect within the art world helped to draw Rockport and Gloucester to the attention of outside artists. Though Gruppe did not come to the region until he was 65, his output was still prolific and he was held in high regard until his death in Rockport in 1940. His son Emile referred to his father as "the great painter" in nearly every art class he taught.

EMILE GRUPPE

1896 — 1978

GRUPPE HAD THE great fortune of being born into a professional, artistic family. His father Charles, born in Canada, had studied in Holland and established a solid reputation as a Barbizon artist in Europe before relocating the family to Rochester, where Emile was later born. There, the Gruppe children were raised surrounded by art and encouraged by their parents.

Young Emile trained under his father for years before studying at the Hague in Holland and later at the Art Students league in New York City. Since the beginning Charles had encouraged Emile's creativity and originality rather than imposing his own approach to painting. From a very early age Emile's style differed from his father's, having a much more spontaneous, Impressionistic approach with a much greater emphasis on color.

It was his meeting with the Woodstock master John F. Carlson in the late 1910's that changed the course of his career. Gruppe spent four years studying with him, developing his techniques in landscape painting. He began to teach some of

Carlson's classes for him and thus began his career in teaching for which he was equally famous and so fondly remembered.

In 1925, during one trip to the Academy he saw examples of work by William Lester Stevens and Frederick Mulhaupt painted on Cape Ann and was immediately motivated to make a trip to the region. Shortly after, Gruppe made the journey with his father and the two lived on Bearskin Neck in Rockport for the next four years. The early Rockport harbor scene entitled *Rockport Inner Harbor* is a rare example of this period. By 1929 Emile had established a studio on Rocky Neck in East Gloucester, and became a very popular teacher.

It is possible that Emile Gruppe was one of the best teachers to ever work in Cape Ann. He was known throughout his life for his generosity and care as a teacher and for his benevolence towards students and buyers especially during the Depression years. In later decades former students of his reminisced about Gruppe's kindness in inviting students in to his classes who could not afford them.

In 1942 Gruppe founded the Gruppe Summer School in Gloucester with his former teacher John F. Carlson. He took trips to Vermont, Florida and even to Portugal, intrigued by the differences and the similarities in the fishermen's life of the two coasts. But Gruppe's home was always Cape Ann. He came to know many of the local fishermen and even took up fishing. He consistently maintained a productive output of work, teaching all the while, often taking students with him on vacations and trips throughout America and Europe. It is said that he painted almost everyday of his life.

Rockport Inner Harbor
CA. 1925 OIL ON CANVAS 14 1/4" X 14 1/4"
PRIVATE COLLECTION
PHOTO COURTESY OF DAVIES FINE ARTS

Gloucester Docks

CA. 1945 OIL ON CANVAS 25" X 30"

PRIVATE COLLECTION

ANTHONY THIEME

1888 - 1954

ANTHONY THIEME has often been regarded as having done more to popularize the Cape Ann region than any other single artist. He was a very prolific painter who produced an enormous body of work and is believed to have painted Motif No. 1 more times than any other painter before or since. He spent a great deal of his artistic life exploring the possibilities of light and the ways in which it affected a wet street, a harbor or a landscape; he has been dubbed the "Master of Sunlight and Shadow." Thieme was an artist who painted rustic outdoor tableaus enfused with the glow of sunlight, but he was also a complex man who not only wrestled with the highs and lows of an artistic life, but also with his own emotional issues.

Born Antonius Johannes Thieme in Rotterdam, Holland, the young man showed an early ability in art and was taking courses at the Academy of Rotterdam from as early as fourteen years old. Despite this however, his parents had little inclination to allow him to pursue the unstable life of a painter and forced him to join a naval school. This began the first of many struggles Thieme contended with throughout his life. Spending time around boats and all their equipment seemed only to heighten Thieme's fascination for this subject as an artist. For a while Thieme

Rockport Shore
CA. 1940'S OIL ON CANVAS 25" X 30"
PRIVATE COLLECTION
PHOTO COURTESY OF THE COOLEY GALLERY

(OPPOSITE)
The Blue Door
CA. 1940'S OIL ON CANVAS 30" X 36"
COLLECTION OF CAPE ANN HISTORICAL ASSOCIATION

studied at the Royal Academy in The Hague, but the irreconcilable differences with his stubborn parents resulted in Thieme permanently leaving home at the age of seventeen.

Over the next several years Thieme studied in Germany, Switzerland, Italy and France, working in stage design painting backdrops to support himself. In 1917 he made the trip to the U.S., changing his name to Anthony. He painted in and around Boston and New York, crisscrossing back and forth from Europe, even making a trip to Brazil and Argentina. Fate brought him to Cape Ann for the first time in 1929, having learned about the area from his Boston contacts and the North Shore Art Association. Shortly after arriving, Thieme met Lillian Beckett and the two married and settled in Rockport.

In 1930 Thieme started the Thieme School of Art on Cape Ann which he ran until 1943. His love and reputation for outdoor painting were already well known and he became a fixture in the area, painting in any weather, even cutting a hole in the floor of his "woodie" station wagon, as the legend goes, so he could stand up and paint in the worst of weather conditions. It was in these years that Thieme's numerous renderings of Motif # 1 and the many other sites of the region spread the fame of Cape Ann across America and even to Europe. He held several exhibitions, won many awards and became one of the most successful painters of the region. On occasion Thieme was accused of being too commercial. It is said, while setting up his easel to paint, a fellow artist noted his blank canvas already had a price tag of $400 written on the stretcher.

In the mid 1940's, the Thieme's bought a home in St. Augustine, Florida where they spent the winter months from then on. Despite gaining more acclaim and success than most artists could ever hope for, Thieme still suffered from personal issues that he was never able to reconcile. He often felt great despair at the evolution of modern life, technology and progress. Today one can only guess at the forces that culminated in Thieme taking his own life during a trip to Florida during an overnight stay at a hotel in Greenwich, Connecticut.

Harbor Reflections
CA. MID 1930'S OIL ON CANVAS 30" X 40"
PRIVATE COLLECTION
PHOTO COURTESY OF DE VILLE GALLERIES

(OPPOSITE)
The Old Salt Barque
CA. MID 1930'S OIL ON CANVAS 36" X 30"
COLLECTION OF THE ROCKPORT
ART ASSOCIATION

GORDON GRANT
1875 – 1962

THERE IS PERHAPS no other American artist who worked in both commercial and fine arts whose paintings are more associated with the great square riggers on the open seas than those of Gordon Grant. His pictures are at once a celebration, a salute and a memorial to every facet of life at sea. When Grant's father sent him from their home in San Francisco to Scotland for schooling via the Horn of South America, the four and a half month journey solidified Grant's growing fascination with shipping and boating. Later studies came in London before Grant returned to America where he served on the Mexican border in the National Guard. In 1895 he began working for publications such as *The Examiner* and later illustrated for *The Chronicle, Journal* and *Harper's Weekly*. With these and other magazines he received fascinating assignments like covering the Boer War in South Africa in 1899.

But as Grant's commercial success grew he finally resolved to focus on marine and nautical images. Grant's picture *Old Ironsides*, poster prints of which were sold in large numbers to pay for the ship's restoration, now hangs in the White House. Grant's commissioned illustration work was of such a high quality that it often bears the look of a pure easel painting. His academic, realist approach is still quite original and always has an earthy gusto. Grant wrote and illustrated a number of his own books and stories.

Painting in the harbors of Cape Ann was only natural for Grant, and he spent several years returning to the region, working from a studio on Rocky Neck; many of his best pictures were painted in Gloucester, such as the massive *Gloucester Harbor*. Grant captured the energy of the harbor during the last days of the enormous square riggers with high masts and full sail. Considered by some to be his finest work, *Gloucester Harbor* is a testament to Grant's working knowledge of the construction and rigging of boats and his ability to render them in detail, yet it also achieves movement, energy and mood using a variety of looser, impressionistic brushwork and wonderful dark and light contrasts.

Dock Side Politics
1945 WATERCOLOR 15" X 20 1/2"
THE COLLECTION OF STORY PARSONS

(OPPOSITE TOP)
Gloucester Harbor
CA. MID 1930'S OIL ON CANVAS 40" X 50"
PRIVATE COLLECTION
PHOTO COURTESY OF VOSE GALLERIES

(OPPOSITE BOTTOM)
Gloucester Tug
CA. 1940 WATERCOLOR 16" X 20"
PRIVATE COLLECTION
PHOTO COURTESY OF DAVIES FINE ARTS

JOHN CORBINO

1905 – 1964

WHEN CRITICS OF the time sought descriptions for the classical, Baroque quality in much of Corbino's work, they most often compared his monumental, figurative style to the European masters Delacroix or Gericault. Truly there was something about his frenzied pictures of human struggle in storms or disaster that bore a resemblance to early romantic paintings from France or Italy. This style was uncommon on Cape Ann; once he was described as the Rubens of New England, and the moniker stuck.

Corbino had come from his birthplace in Vittoria, Italy at the age of eight to stay with family in New York. An earthquake in Italy and a hurricane he experienced while at sea are believed to have greatly influenced the struggling, dramatic quality of his paintings. At seventeen Corbino attended the Pennsylvania Academy of Fine Arts, studying under George Luks and Frank Vincent DuMond. His first visits to Cape Ann occurred in the early 1930's, but it was not until he was awarded a grant from the Guggenheim to work in Rockport that he moved there in 1936. Corbino spent the next twenty summers painting on the Cape. When not at his easel he could always be seen painting something; he painted murals on the walls of his home as well as those of his friends. He enjoyed festive occasions, often having dinners or parties where he was still inclined to paint, whether it was live studies of the gathering, or caricatures, such as a Last Supper spoof made up of Max Kuehne and his family and friends. These pictures would often remain a permanent part of the home. Decades later, new owners would move into these houses only to find remarkable murals on the walls.

For many years Corbino worked in this neo-baroque, romantic manner. He transformed the crashing surf, the drama of fishermen battling the ocean into a struggle of man and the elements that had an almost Biblical monumentality. Even his peaceful images of picnics and festivities had an allegorical quality. Such images brought Corbino wide acclaim; he was featured in a *Life* magazine article simply titled "Corbino is the Rubens of New England."

Down East Home
1938 OIL ON CANVAS 30" X 40"
PRIVATE COLLECTION
PHOTO COURTESY OF BABCOCK GALLERY

STOW WENGENROTH
1906 - 1978

STOW WENGENROTH was a major American lithographer whom Andrew Wyeth called "the greatest black and white artist in America."[44] He was equally adept at rendering street scenes with architectural precision, animal images of zoological accuracy, sunny harbor pictures, dark and ominous night scenes or World War II aircraft - always with an uncanny mastery for capturing mood, light and surface texture.

Born in Brooklyn, Wengenroth's father was an architect; his mother, a textile designer. By high school he had shown an aptitude for art and was enrolled in the Art Student's League in 1923. In 1925 he studied at the Grand Central School of Art, spending his summers training with John Carlson in Woodstock, NY. In Eastport, Maine he studied with George Ennis. It was Ennis who first suggested lithography to

Wengenroth, and by 1929 he was producing his first works in the medium.

Wengenroth had found his calling and went about this new craft with great energy, lugging 75 pound lithographic stones back and forth from his printer's office to work on them at home. With his wife, Edith, the two spent the next several decades making frequent trips from New Jersey to New Hampshire, capturing what is most picturesque, eerie, peculiar and endearing about New England. But a great majority of his work was produced either in Maine or on Cape Ann. He and his wife visited there every year throughout his career. Wengenroth once said:

"I love Cape Ann most of all for its quiet beauty.....
Seaward, five lighthouses make the approaches to the
Cape's various harbors. The outer side of the land is

Gloucester Days
1947 DRYBRUSH DRAWING 13" X 24"
PRIVATE COLLECTION

(OPPOSITE)

Tuck's Drugstore
CA. 1940'S DRYBRUSH DRAWING 14" X 20"
PRIVATE COLLECTION

hilly. Inland, the little Annisquam River wanders calmly and peacefully to the sea, and technically speaking, makes the Cape an island. Long stretches of flat land, broken by inlets and coves, add variety to the scene that has for years lured artists from all parts of the country."[45]

Except for a brief period early in his career working with Andrew Wyeth in the watercolor medium, Wengenroth focused completely on lithography. Towards the end of his life however, at the suggestion of friends, he did again try his hand at color, producing mostly watercolor still-lifes. As tightly executed as his lithographs, they showed various kinds of fabric, almost always a few beautifully sculpted flowers, often carnations, and a butterfly, the symbol of resurrection.

However, it was his lithographs that made his name as an artist. His work was sold both commercially and as fine prints. Like his predecessor to the region, Stephen Parrish, he helped to popularize Cape Ann through the sale of affordable prints, especially during the Depression years. He was also an adept writer, penning *Making a Lithograph*, an in-depth analysis on the production and techniques of the medium. He worked steadily until the last year of his life, dying in Rockport in 1978.

TED KAUTZKY

1896 – 1953

THOUGH LESS IS known of Kautzky's career than some of his contemporaries, he made a profound impact both on Cape Ann and nationally. His book, *Ways with Watercolor*, published in 1949 was one of the best selling instructional books of its kind. It has also been regarded as one of the first comprehensive works on the watercolor medium produced after World War II, used by both students and art teachers alike.

Born in Budapest, Hungary, Kautzky studied architecture at the Royal University of Hungary and, after receiving his degree, made his way to the United States in 1923. He taught at the Pratt Institute, New York University and at the University of Pennsylvania and became a U.S. citizen in 1929.

Kautzky was a master of watercolor—his control and ability to render textures, colors, light reflection and tone with one spontaneous but perfectly placed stroke is uncanny. Painted in 1950, *Tidal Flats*, is an extraordinary example of

this skill. Kautzky's image is nothing short of mesmerizing. Working with a careful consideration of light reflection, the picture's monochromatic fields of blue become hypnotic. Without tapping into any of the usual social or political subjects that 'make people think,' Kautzky creates an image that inspires contemplation. He shows the viewer a cerebral, almost cosmic setting that seems so otherworldly that to describe it as simply a coastal picture would seem too baroque, too simple a description. The boat looks almost marooned on an alien planet, set amidst a landscape that is neither liquid nor solid, veiled in darkness yet full of light, absent and barren yet still full of the richness of nature.

Kautzky spent more than a decade on Cape Ann. He was a member of the National Academy of Design, the Rockport Art Association, the North Shore Arts Association and the American Watercolor Society, among many others. He won numerous awards for his pictures.

The Hannah Jumper House
WATERCOLOR 22" X 30"
PRIVATE COLLECTION
PHOTO COURTESY OF DAVIES FINE ARTS

Tidal Flats
1950 WATERCOLOR 22" X 30"
PRIVATE COLLECTION
PHOTO COURTESY OF DAVIES FINE ARTS

NELL BLAINE

1922 – 1996

IN 1942, at the age of nineteen, Nell Blaine came to New York from Richmond, Virginia to study with Hans Hoffman. Competent in representational art from previous studies at the Richmond Professional Institute, the nature of her work radically changed after settling in Manhattan. Surrounded by artists like Leland Bell, Louisa Matthiasdottir, and Al Kresch, Blaine was very active in the burgeoning New York modern art scene. Like Stuart Davis, Nell Blaine's exposure to jazz had an enormous impact on her work. The music encouraged experimentation, innovation and revolution in many artists and writers throughout the era. Her studio became a gathering place for painters and musicians; she once had the courage to approach Charlie Parker at a club to invite him to her studio.

Blaine appeared to be a committed abstract painter, working in geometric and biomorphic shapes often against a white background, and yet by the early 1950's her work was becoming figurative and representational once again. Her first trip to Cape Ann came in 1943, and by the early 50's, she was spending the summers in Gloucester.

In 1959 she took an extended trip to the Mediterranean where she traveled to Italy, Greece, Turkey and Egypt.

After several months of painting on the Greek Island of Mykonos, she fell ill and began exhibiting the symptoms of bulbar-spinal polio. After a harrowing and prolonged evacuation back to the United States, she was hospitalized for seven months. Paralyzed in the legs and partially in the arms, she was told by doctors that not only would she never walk again, but also that she might never again paint. Blaine began practicing painting with her left hand before a long regimen of surgery and rehabilitation gave her back the use of her right hand.

Her doctors had expected that she would die and at times had even brought priests in to offer her last rights. And yet within a year's time, after release from the hospital she was not only painting again but stepped up her travel and exhibition schedule. Over the next several years she traveled and painted in upstate New York, France, Spain, Portugal, England and lived for five months on St. Lucia in the Caribbean.

Red Candle and Four Bouquets
1978 OIL ON CANVAS 26" X 30"
COURTESY OF TIBOR DE NAGY
TRANSPARENCY BY O.E. NELSON

Loblolly Cove
1982 WATERCOLOR 18" X 24"
COLLECTION OF A. COHEN
COURTESY OF TIBOR DE NAGY
TRANSPARENCY BY O.E. NELSON

Bound to a wheelchair, Blaine often painted scenes from her backyard or views from a studio window. She made several return trips to Cape Ann in the intervening years until she bought a home on the coast of Gloucester in 1974. There she would spend five months a year, each year until her death in 1996. The body of work created in this atmosphere shaped the look and style for which Blaine is most well known today. Working in both oil and watercolor, she painted bright, uplifting images of harbors, landscapes and still-lifes with intense color and light. Her use of both mediums was unconventional and original. Often her oils have a wash quality usually found in watercolor, while her watercolors attain a richness of color often only found in oil.

Up until her death Blaine remained intensely active on all fronts. Winner of many awards, including the Krasner Award from the Pollock-Krasner foundation, over her lifetime she held fifty-four solo exhibitions of her work. While her handicap must never be used to define her as an artist, like other Cape Ann painters Marguerite Pearson and Fitz Hugh Lane, Nell Blaine's permanent disability must also never be overlooked when admiring a picture and pondering the nature of its creation.

AL CZEREPAK

1928 - 1986

"THERE ARE PROBABLY as many anecdotes as there are Czerepak artworks,"[46] described Westin Boer in the Gloucester Times. An outsider in Cape Ann in terms of his aesthetic pursuits, there are few artists in the region who have been remembered more fondly than Al Czerepak. His artwork was as experimental and improvisational as his personality was down to earth and compassionate. Firmly rooted in traditional training, Czerepak worked in practically every medium and mode over his life, unabashed in his curiosity to work in any style with any objects, surfaces or materials that could serve his purpose. Like Picasso, no objects or mediums were off limits. He worked in oils, painted frescoes, carved wood, welded scrap metal "and other detritus of the 20th century"[47] and searched beaches and nearby dumps looking for unique objects that would ultimately find themselves converted to art.

The son of Polish immigrants, Czerepak studied art at the Vesper George School of Art and later at the Massachusetts School of Art, graduating in 1955. Further training at the Academia di Belle Arti in Florence, Italy and at the Instituto Allende in Mexico greatly expanded Czerepak's range of style and influence. He also traveled extensively throughout Eastern Europe, the Mediterranean and the Middle East, but it was his Polish heritage that Czerepak continued to draw upon throughout his life.

Czerepak taught for several years at the Montserrat School of Art. To study a selection of his work is to be astounded that they were rendered by the same hand. He was at once a folk artist, a modernist, an expressionist, a sculptor, a conceptual artist and a portrait painter. Czerepak most likely first came to Cape Ann in the early 1950's. Friendly, compassionate and encouraging, Boer recalls that "his studio was like a village crossroads."[48] He taught art to local children and was eventually dubbed the "pied piper of Rockport." Truly a kindred spirit, Boer wrote of him, "Like the American Indian, he believed in the Great Spirit; and like the Polish Catholic he was born, he loved the simple humility of the faithful, the pageantry of the faith itself, the majesty of its music and art, and the cosmic mystery of its long lost roots."[49]

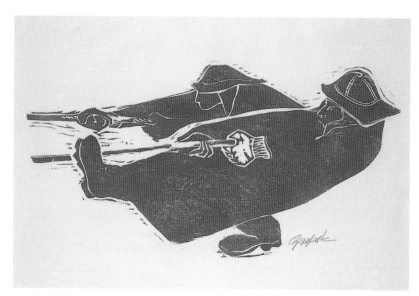

Snugging Up
BLOCK PRINT 16" X 27"
COLLECTION OF MARILYN RASMUSSEN

(OPPOSITE)
The Violist
CA. 1972 OIL ON CANVAS 23" X 17"
PRIVATE COLLECTION

PAUL STRISIK

1918 – 1998

AT 27 YEARS OLD, Paul Strisik, a veteran of the Second World War, frustrated with his start-up business, finally resolved to become a painter. Born in Brooklyn, he had grown up always working with his hands, absorbed in hobbies like gem-cutting, photography and fishing. In these years he always saw paintings in magazines and museums but pursued other interests. Strisik served for four years in the Navy during the Second World War. Stationed in North Africa, he became a Chief Photographer's Mate, and while shooting in French Morocco for *Life* magazine, his exposure to the desert landscape restimulated his passion for the visual arts. Like many who served in the war, upon returning home Strisik was determined to make up for lost time.

Firm in his aspiration to be an artist, he briefly took up studies with an abstract painter. He soon stopped, later explaining,

"He said personal experience was what was important. I asked him once if I should not at least be able to do a traditional portrait or landscape, even though we were painting abstractly. He told me that not knowing how to do such things was an advantage, because I had nothing to unlearn.....I was very unhappy because there were many paintings in museums I loved and I knew that what this man was teaching me would never lead me to those paintings. But Frank Vincent DuMond would lead me there."[50]

Thus, contrary to the modernist trend that swept through America after World War II, Strisik joined the academic tradition. On the GI Bill, he began studying with DuMond at the Art Students League. DuMond, then 80, had sat on exhibition juries with Winslow Homer; a living legend of the past, he was an artist, teacher and philosopher that infused Strisik with the knowledge and

The Sapphire Jar
1991 OIL ON CANVAS 24" X 20"
COLLECTION OF MR. AND MRS. JOHN B. PRENTISS

(OPPOSITE)
Evening Tide, Gloucester
1974 OIL ON CANVAS 20" X 30"
STRISIK COLLECTION

wisdom he sought. Strisik became enthralled with plein air painting, and after later sessions with his friend Robert Lougheed, pursued landscape and still-lifes, favoring oriental subjects.

Strisik came to Rockport in 1952. Having first learned of the town from a magazine article he had read as a child, Strisik would become a pillar of the art colony, serving as president of the Rockport Art Association, teaching and keeping a gallery of his work, which at the time of his death, was and still is the longest running gallery in the town. An avid traveler, Strisik journeyed and painted throughout Europe, the Caribbean, Canada and Mexico, and fell in love with painting in the Southwest.

A member of the National Academy of Design, Strisik won over 180 awards during his career, wrote two books, including *The Art of Landscape*

Painting and was featured in several TV appearances. Like Aldro T. Hibbard before him, Strisik was outspoken in protecting the town and the art colony, speaking out against the spread of mass produced, assembly line art in the region. A traditionalist all his life, Strisik mixed both the brisk work of outdoor painting, on location, and the more careful, contemplative work of the studio. He continued the tradition of inventive and imaginative, but academically trained art, expanding it through years of travel, open-minded to painting a variety of locations, subjects and mediums, always however, knowing the limitations.

"Painting is extremely limited compared to nature's power," he once said. "We are not working with the things the Good Lord is working with—we don't have light, dark, close and far, we only have paint...."[51]

Blessing of The Fleet, Gloucester
1988 OIL ON CANVAS 36" X 48"
COURTESY OF THE PEABODY ESSEX MUSEUM, SALEM, MA

1. *Painters of Cape Ann*, Spanierman Gallery, 1996.
2. Wilmerding, *Paintings by Fitz Hugh Lane*, p. 19.
3. Baur, *Antiques The Magazine*, Nov. 1980: p. 1025.
4. Sharf, *Hunt and the Summer Art Colony at Magnolia*, p. 10.
5. Cooley, *Rockport Sketchbook*, p. 19.
6. ibid.
7. Butler, *The Artist as Historian*, 1983.
8. ibid.
9. Gerdts, *Childe Hassam*, p. 107-108.
10. Gerdts, *Lasting Impressions*, p. 51.
11. Royal Cortissoz, *The Virile Art of The Late Eric Hudson*.
12. *Eric Hudson, 1864–1932*, p. 3.
13. *Willard Leroy Metcalf*, Springfield Museum of Fine Arts, p. xiii.
14. *Edward Potthast*, New York: Chapellier Galleries.
15. Falk, *Who was Who in American Art*, Vol. 1, p. 252.
16. *The Glow of Sunlight*, Vose Galleries, 1998.
17. Cooley, *Rockport Sketch Book*, p. 22.
18. Movalli, *American Artist*, p. 75.
19. ibid.
20. *Paintings by Frederick Waugh*, 1968.
21. ibid.
22. Havens, *Frederick J. Waugh*, p. 122.
23. Levin, *Edward Hopper: An Intimate Biography*, p. 169.
24. *John Sloan: The Gloucester Years*, 1980.
25. ibid.
26. *Hayley Lever*, Previti Gallery, 1985.
27. Wilkin, *Stuart Davis in Gloucester*, p. 4o.
28. *Theresa Bernstein*, Joan Whalen Gallery, p. 8.
29. Charles Movalli, "A New View of Aldro T. Hibbard," *American Artist* (May 1979): p.60.
30. Thomas Davies, "A.T. Hibbard, A Retrospective," *American Art Review* (Oct 1996): p. 146.
31. "Painter of New England Winters," *American Artist*, (June 1940): p. 8.
32. Davies, p. 149.
33. ibid.
34. ibid, p.147.
35. Carr, *American Art Review*, p. 119.
36. Marsden Hartley, *Soliloquy in Dogtown*, 1985, p. 21.
37. ibid, p. 9.
38. ibid, p. 14.
39. ibid, p. 13.
40. Cooley, *Rockport Sketch Book*, p. 55.
41. *Antiques and the Arts Weekly*, July 15, 1988, p. 18.
42. Curtis, *American Art Review*, April 2000: 187.
43. Cooley, *Rockport Sketch Book*, p. 69.
44. Davies, *Inspiration of Cape Ann*, p. 27.
45. Stuckey, *The Lithographs of Stow Wengenroth*, p. 18
46. Westin Boer, "A Tribute to Cape Ann Art, Al Czerepak" *Gloucester Daily Times*, (Aug. 28, 1986)
47. ibid.
48. ibid.
49. ibid.
50. Murphy, *The Santa Fean Magazine*, Sept., 1990, p. 61.
51. ibid., p. 62.

BIBLIOGRAPHY

A

A Century and a Half of American Art 1825 – 1975. New York: National Academy of Design, 1975.

"Aldro T. Hibbard: Painter of New England." *American Artist*. June 1940: 8 –11.

American and European Paintings under $7500 . Exhibition Catalogue. Philadelphia: Schwarz, 1993.

American Collection. Hickory Museum of Art. Hickory: The Hickory Printing Group, 1994.

American Impressionist and Realist Paintings & Drawings. New York: Metropolitan Museum of Art, 1973.

American Painters of the Impressionist Period Rediscovered. Exhibition Catalogue. Colby College Art Museum, 1975.

American Paintings . New York: Berry Hill Gallery, 1990.

American Paintings in the Boston Museum of Fine Arts. 2 Vols. Boston: Museum of Fine Arts, 1969.

The Art of Carl William Peters.. Chicago: R.H. Love Galleries, 1994.

The Art of Collecting. Exhibition Catalogue. New York: Hirschl & Adler Galleries, Inc., 1984.

Artists of the Rockport Art Association: 1956. Gloucester: Rockport Art Association, 1956.

Artists of the Rockport Art Association: 1970. Gloucester: Rockport Art Association, 1970.

Atkinson, D. Scott and Jochen Wierich. *Winslow Homer in Gloucester*. Exhibition Catalogue. Chicago: Terra Museum of American Art, 1990.

B

Baekeland, Frederick. *Images of America: The Painter'e Eye, 1833 – 1925*. Birmingham Museum of Art, 1991.

---, *Roads Less Traveled: American Paintings, 1833 – 1935*. Ithaca: Herbert F. Johnson Museum of Art, 1998.

Banks, Marissa., Lorraine Glennon and Jeffrey Schaire. "The 25 Most Undervalued American Artists." *Art & Antiques*. Oct. 1986: 63 – 81.

Baur, John I.H. "Francis A. Silva: Beyond Luminism."*Antiques The Magazine*. Nov 1980: 1018 – 1031.

Beam, Philip C. *Winslow Homer at Prout's Neck* . Boston: Little, Brown & Co., 1966.

Boyle, Richard J. *American Impressionism*. Boston: New York Graphic Society, 1974.

---, *John Twachtman*. New York: Watson-Guptill Pub.,1979.

Butler, Joyce. *The Artist as Historian: Augustus W. Buhler 1853 – 1920* . Gloucester: Cape Ann Historical Society, 1983.

Bressler, Sidney. *Reynolds Beal*. Rutherford: Fairleigh Dickinson University Press, 1989.

Burke, Doreen Bolger. *American Paintings in the Metropolitan Museum of Art* . Vol. 3. New York: Princeton Univ. Press, 1980.

C

Carl W. Peters. Exhibition Catalogue. New York: Spanierman Gallery, LLC., 1998.

Carl W. Peters. Los Angeles: DeVille Galleries, 1986.

Carr, Gerald L. "Hugh Henry Breckenridge: A Philadelphia Modernist." *American Art Review* . May 1978: 92 – 99.

A Century of American Illustration. Exhibition Catalogue. New York: The Brooklyn Museum of Art, 1972.

Childe Hassam . Exhibition Catalogue. New York: Bernard Danenberg Galleries, Inc.

Childe Hassam . Exhibition Catalogue. New York: Spanierman Gallery, 1988.

Childe Hassam . Exhibition Catalogue. East Hampton: Guild Hall, 1967.

Christie's New York: Important American Paintings, Drawings and Sculptures . Tuesday Nov. 30 1999: 11.

A Circle of Friends: Art Colonies of Cornish and Dublin. Exhibition Catalogue. University Art Galleries, Univ. of New Hampshire, 1985.

Clark, Marion Dodge. "Maurice Compris, Portrait Painter and Muralist Passes Away." *Gloucester Times*. 20 Oct. 1939.

Cooley, John L. *A.T. Hibbard, N.A.: Artists in Two Worlds*. Concord: The Rumford Press, 1968.

---, *Rockport Sketch Book*. Rockport: Rockport Art Association, 1965.

Corbin, Kathryn. "John Leslie Breck, American Impressionist." *Antiques The Magazine* Nov. 1988: 1142-1149.

Corbino on Cape Ann: The Rubens of New England. Gloucester: Cape Ann Historical Museum, 1995.

Cortissoz, Royal. "The Virile Art of the Late Eric Hudson." *Herald Tribune*.

Curtis, Jane., Will Curtis and Frank Lieberman. *Monhegan Island The Artists' Island* . Camden: Down East Books, 1995.

Curtis, Judith. *Anthony Thieme*. Rockport: Rockport Art Association, 1999.

---, "Exponents of the Boston School." *American Art Review*. April 2000: 186 – 193.

---, "Images of a New England Seacoast." *American Art Review*. Oct 1998: 232-247.

D

Davies, Thomas G. *The Inspiration of Cape Ann*. Rockport Art Association.

---, "Aldro T. Hibbard, N.A.: A Retrospective." *American Art Review*. Oct. 1996: 142 – 149.

---, *The Artists' Choice: The Land, The Sea, The People*. Rockport Art Association.

Davis, Earl. *Stuart Davis: Scapes* . Exhibition Catalogue. New York: Slander- O'Reilly Galleries, 1990.

Domit, Moussa M. *American Impressionist Painting*. Washington: National Gallery of Art, 1973.

E

The Early Paintings of Max Kuehne. Exhibition Catalogue. New York: Hirschl & Adler Galleries Inc., 1972.

Edward Hopper : Early and Late. Exhibition Catalogue. New York: Hirschl & Adler, 1987.

Edward Henry Potthast New York: Chapellier Galleries.

Edward Henry Potthast: American Impressionist. Exhibition Catalogue. New York: Gerald Peters Gallery, 1998.

Emile A. Gruppe" A Retrospective. Exhibition Catalogue. Gloucester: North Shore Art Association, 1997.

Ellen Day Hale . Exhibition Catalogue. New York: Richard York Gallery, 1981.

F

Fairbrother, Trevor J. *The Bostonians Painters of an Elegant Age, 1870 – 1930*. Boston: Museum of Fine Arts, 1986.

Falk, Peter Hastings. *Who was Who in American Art 1564 – 1975* . 3 Vols. Madison: Sound View Press, 1999.

Fink, Lois Marie. *American Art at the Nineteenth Century Paris Salons* . New York: Cambrdige Univ. Press, 1990.

Fitz Hugh Lane . Exhibition Catalogue. Rockland: The William A. Farnsworth Library and Art Museum, 1974.

Foster, Kathleen A. "Winslow Homer: A Personal View." *American Art Review*. May 1996: 92 – 95.

Frank Duveneck. Exhibition Catalogue. New York: Chapellier Galleries, 1972.

Frank Duveneck: The Gloucester Years, 1892 – 1917. Exhibition Catalogue. New York: David Findlay Jr Inc.

Frank Duveneck: The Gloucester Years. Gloucester: Cape Ann Historical Association, 1987.

Frederick J. Mulhaupt: A Reintroduction. Exhibition Catalogue. Boston: Vose Galleries, 1978.

Frederick J. Mulhaupt: Dean of the Cape Ann School. Gloucester: North Shore Arts Association, 1999.

Frederick J. Waugh. Exhibition Catalogue. New York: Kennedy Galleries, 1978.

Frederick J. Waugh. New York: Grand Central Art Galleries, 1936.

French Impressionists Influence American Artists. Exhibition Catalogue. Coral Gables, Lowe Art Museum, Univ. of Miami, 1971.

G

Gallatin, A.E. "Max Kuehne, Cosmopolite." *International Studio*. April 1924: 58 – 62.

Gallery Glimpses. Vol. 2, Issue 1. Atlanta: Peachtree Gallery, 1985.

Gammel, R.H. Ives. *The Boston Painters 1900 – 1930*. Orleans: Parnassus Imprints, 1986.

Gardner, Albert Van Eyck. *Winslow Homer American Artist: His World and His Work*. New York: Bramhall House, 1961.

George L. Noyes/ Charles H. Woodbury. Exhibition Catalogue. Boston: Vose Galleries of Boston, Inc., 1987.

George W. Harvey: Images of Cape Ann and Beyond. Exhibition Catalogue. Newburyport: Lepore Fine Arts, 1991.

Gerdts, William H. *American Impressionism*. New York: Abbeville Press, 1984.

---, *American Impressionism*. Seattle: The Henry art Gallery, 1980.

---, *Lasting Impressions American Painters in France, 1815 – 1915*. Musée Americain, Giverny: Terra Foundation for the Arts, 1992.

---, *Masterworks of American Impressionism from the Pfeil Collection*. Alexandria: Art Services International, 1992.

---, *Art Across America* . Vol 1. New York: Abbeville Press, 1990.

---, *Childe Hassam Impressionist* . New York: Abbeville Press, 1999.

Gifford Beal. Exhibition Catalogue. Mountainville: The Storm King Art Center, 1968.

Gifford Beal. Exhibition Catalogue. Washington: Montclair Art Museum,1972.

Gifford Beal. Exhibition Catalogue. New York: Kraushaar Galleries, 1965.

Gifford Beal: At The Water's Edge. Exhibition Catalogue. New York: Kraushaar Galleries, 2000.

The Glorious Quest . New York: Godel & Co., 1998.

Gloucester at Mid-Century: The World of Fitz Hugh Lane. Gloucester: Cape Ann Historical Association, 1989.

Gloucester: Views of the Art Colony by American Masters. Exhibition Catalogue. Chicago: R.H. Love Galleries, Inc., 1991.

The Glow of Sunlight: Paintings by George L. Noyes.. Boston: Vose Galleries, 1998.

Goodrich, Lloyd. *Edward Hopper*. New York: Harry N. Abrams, Inc., 1993.

---, *Edward Hopper* . New York: Whitney Museum of American Art, 1971.

---, *Winslow Homer* . New York: George Braziller, Inc. 1959.

---, *Winslow Homer* . Exhibition Catalogue. New York: Whitney Museum of American Art, 1973.

H

H. Boylston Dummer: New England Impressionist . Exhibition Catalogue. Essex: Marine Arts Gallery.

Hale, John Douglass., Richard J. Boyle, and William H. Gerdts. *Twachtman in Gloucester: His Last Years, 1900-1902*. Exhibition Catalogue. New York: Ira Spanierman Gallery 1987

---, Lisa N Peters, William H. Gerdts, anf Richard J. Boyle. *In the Sunlight: The Floral and Figurative Art of J.H. Twachtman*. Exhibition Catalogue. New York: Ira Spanierman Gallery, 1989.

Harriet Randall Lumis: 1870 – 1953. Exhibition Catalogue. Chicago: R.H. Love Galleries, 1977.

Harriet Randall Lumis: Grande Dame of Landscape Painting. Chicago: R.H. Love Galleries, 1989.

Havens, George R. *Frederick J. Waugh: American Marine Painter*. Orono: University of Maine Press, 1969.

Hayley Lever: Selected Works c. 1900 – 1933. Exhibition Catalogue. New York: Bernard Black Gallery

Hayley Lever: A Retrospective. Exhibition Catalogue. New York: Previti Gallery, 1985.

Hayley Lever: American Impressionist. New Canaan, Hastings Art Ltd., 1985.

Hendricks, Gordon. *The Life and Work of Winslow Homer*. New York: Harry N. Abrams, Inc., Publishers, 1979.

Heisinger, Ulrich W. *Childe Hassam American Impressionist*. Munich: Prestel, 1999.

Hoopes, Donelson F. *The American Impressionists*. New York: Watson-Guptil Publications, 1972.

I

"Rockport and Gloucester." *Illuminator*. Spring 1978: 15 – 16.

An Itinerant Spirit: The Early Works of Jane Peterson. Exhibition Catalogue. Hirschl & Adler Galleries, Inc., 1995.

J

Jane Peterson. Exhibition Catalogue. New York: Hirschl & Adler Galleries, Inc., 1970.

Jane Peterson/ Hayley Lever Jane Peterson. Exhibition Catalogue. New York: H.V. Allison Galleries, 1990.

John Henry Twachtman. Exhibition Catalogue. New York: Ira Spanierman, 1968.

John Sloan. Exhibition Catalogue. Hanover: Hood Museum of Art, 1982.

John Sloan: The Gloucester Years. New York: Kraushaar Galleries.

K

Kautzky, Ted. *Ways With Watercolor* . New York: Reinhold Publishing Co., 1949.

Keny, James M. *Legacy of Cape Ann*. Exhibition Catalogue. Canton: Canton Museum of Fine Arts, 1995.

---, "The Legacy of Cape Ann." *American Art Review*. Oct-Nov 1995: 128 – 133.

Kienholz, Katheen. "Frederick J. Mulhaupt." *American Art Review*. Aug 1999: 114 – 123.

Kristiansen, Rolf H., and John J. Leahy. *Rediscovering Some New England Artists: 1875 – 1900*. Dedham: Gardner-O'Brien Associates, 1987.

L

Larson, Judy L., Donelson Hoopes and Phyllis Peet. *American Paintings in the High Museum of Art*. New York: Hudson Hills Press, 1994.

Leon Kroll . Exhibition Catalogue. Boston: Judi Rotenberg Gallery & Art Research Associates, Inc.,

Leon Kroll Revisited . New York: Gerald Peters Gallery, 1998.

Levin, Gail. *Edward Hopper: An Intinate Biography*. New York: Knopf, 1995.

Little, Carl. *Winslow Homer and the Sea*. San Francisco: Pomegranate Art Books, 1995.

Love, R.H. *Carl W. Peters : American Scene Painter from Rochester to Rockport* . New York: University of Rochester, 1999.

M

MacAdam, Barbara J. *Winter's Promise: Willard Metcalf in Cornish, New Hampshire*. Hood Museum of Art, Dartmouth College, 1999.

Marguerite S. Pearson American Painter. Hingham, Pierce Galleries, Inc.

Marsden Hartley 1877 – 1943. Exhibition Catalogue. Long Island: C.W. Post Gallery, 1977.

Marsden Hartley: Soliloquy in Dogtown . Gloucester: Cape Ann Historical Association, 1985.

Martha Walter. Exhibition Catalogue. Boston: Vose Galleries of Boston, Inc., 1992.

Martha Walter. Exhibition Catalogue. New York: Hammer Galleries, 1969.

Martha Walter. Exhibition Catalogue. New York: Hammer Galleries, 1974.

Martin, Lisa B. "Art For All: The Cape Ann School." *Antiques & Fine Art*. April 1992: 95-101.

Marx, Bill. "Cape Ann's State of Art." *Lynn Magazine*. Jan 1988: 28 – 31.

Masterworks: A 75th Anniversary Survey of Early and Founding Members. Gloucester: North Shore Arts Association, 1997.

Max Kuehne. Exhibition Catalogue. Gloucester: Cape Ann Historical Museum, 1997.

McCauley, Lena M. "The Gallery on the Moors." *The American Magazine of Art*. Nov 1916: 19-20.

McLane, Merrill F. *Place Names of Old Sandy Bay*. Bethesda: Helene Orbaen, 1998.

Mecklenburg, Virginia, M. *Edward Hopper The Watercolors*. New York: W.W. Norton & Co., 1999.

Milton Avery On Cape Ann, Exhibition Catalogue. Gloucester: Cape Ann Historical Association, 1989.

Morris Hall Pancoast. Exhibition Catalogue. Boston: Arvest Galleries, Inc., 1983.

Movalli, Charles. "A New View of Aldro T. Hibbard." *American Artist*. May 1979: 60 –65.

---, "Frederick Mulhaupt: New England Classic." *American Artist*. Jan 1978: 72 – 77.

---, "Lester Stevens." *American Artist*. April 1986: 52 – 56.

---, "Paul Strisik: Inside and Out." *American Artist*. June 1979: 32–37.

Murphy, Francis. *Willard Leroy Metcalf*. Springfield: Museum of Fine Arts, 1976.

Murphy, Joy Waldren. "Paul Strisik, Artist." *The Santa Fean Magazine*. Sept 1990: 60 – 63.

N

Novak, Barbara. *Nineteenth Century American Painting* . New York: Artabras, Abbevillle Pub., 1986.

---, *Next to Nature – Landscape Paintings from the National Academy of Design*. New York: Harper & Row, Pub., 1980.

O

On the Beach: Cape Ann People and Places. Gloucester: Cape Ann Historical Association, 1981.

One Hundred Years on Cape Ann 1840 – 1940. Boston: Vose Galleries of Boston, Inc., 1990.

P

Pagano, Grace. *Contemporary American Painting*. New York: Duel, Sloan and Pierce, 1945.

Painters of Cape Ann, 1840 – 1940: One Hundred Years in Gloucester and Rockport. New York: Spanierman Gallery, 1996.

Paintings by Frederick J. Waugh. Exhibition Catalogue. Trenton: Nw Jersey State Museum, 1968.

The Paintings and Etchings of William Meyerowitz and Theresa Bernstein . Cape Ann Historical Society, 1986.

Paintings by Hayley Lever . Exhibition Catalogue. Farmington: Tom Veilleux Gallery.

Paul Cornoyer: American Impressionist . Peoria: Lakeview Center for the Arts and Sciences, 1973.

Paul Strisik: A Biographical Sketch. Franklin Center, Franklin Mint Gallery of American Art, 1974.

Peters, Lisa N. *Visions of Home American Impressionism Images of Suburban Leisure and Country Comfort*. Exhibition Catalogue. Hanover: University Press of New England, 1997.

Pierce, Patricia Jobe. *Edmund C. Tarbell and the Boston School of Painting* . Hingham: Pierce Galleries Inc., 1980.

Pisano, Ronaldo G. *Gifford Beal: Picture Maker* . Exhibition Catalogue. Muscarelle Museum of Art, College of William and Mary, 1993.

Preato, Robert R. *The Genius of the Fair Muse: Painting and Sculpture Celebrating American Women Artists, 1875 – 1945*. New York: Grand Central Art Galleries, 1987.

---, *Impressionism and Post-Impressionism*. New York: Grand Central Art Galleries, 1988.

R

Radack, Eric. "Spanierman exhibit features Cape Ann artists." *North Shore Magazine*. 22 Feb 1990.

Recchia, Kitty Parsons. *Artists of the Rockport Art Association*. Rockport: Rockport Art Association, 1940.

The Red Cottage. Exhibition Catalogue. Cape Ann Historical Association, 1992.

The Rediscovered Years.- Leon Kroll. New York: Bernard Danenberg Galleries, Inc., 1970.

Reed, Walt., and Roger Reed. *The Illustrator in America 1880 – 1980*. New York: Madison Square Press, 1984.

Reminiscences of Emile Gruppé: The Artist and the Man. Cheshire: Fine Arts Associates of Cheshire, 1992.

Reynolds Beal: Paintings, Drawings and Watercolors . Vose Galleries of Boston, Inc., 1988.

Reynolds Beal. Exhibition Catalogue. Vose Galleries of Boston. Inc., 1983.

Reynolds Beal 1867 – 1951. Exhibition Catalogue. Vose Galleries of Boston, Inc., 1973.

Reynolds Beal . Exhibition Catalogue. Washington: Montclair Museum of Art, 1971.

Reynolds Beal: American Impressionist . Exhibition Catalogue. New York: Hammer Galleries, 1991.

Reynolds Beal: Impressions of an American Artist. Exhibition Catalogue. The Haig Tashjian Collection, Sterling Regal, Inc., 1984.

Roque, Oswaldo Rodriguez. *Directions in American Paintings 1875 – 1925*. Pittsburgh, Museum of Art, Carnegie Institute, 1982.

S

Schjeldahl, Peter. *Edward Hopper: Light Years* . New York: Hirschl & Adler Galleries, Inc., 1988.

Sharf, Frederic A., and John H. Wright. *William Morris Hunt and the Summer Art Colony at Magnolia, Massachusetts 1876 – 1879*. Salem: Essex Institute, 1981.

Shipp, Steve. *American Art Colonies, 1850 – 1930: An Historical Guide to America's Original Art Colonies and Their Artists* . Westport: Greenwood Press, 1996.

Smith, David M. and Jill Warren. "Paul Strisik: Interaction of Heart and Soul." *Southwest Art*. March 1981: 96 – 99.

Some American Painters in Gloucester. Boston: Thomas Todd Co., 1975.

Stein, Roger. "Winslow Homer: The Cultural Work of an Exhibition." *American Art Review*. Aug 1996: 86 – 89.

Stephen Parrish. Exhibtion Catalogue. Gloucester: Cape Ann Historical Association, 1986.

Stephen Parrish. Exhibition Catalogue. Boston: Vose Galleries of Boston, Inc., 1982.

Sternberg Sr., Paul E. *Art by American Women*. Gainesville: Brenau College, 1991.

Stuckey, Ronald., and Joan Stuckey. *The Lithographs of Stow Wengenroth 1931 – 1972*. Boston Public Library, 1974.

---, and Joan Stuckey. *Stow Wengenroth's Lithographs: A Supplement*. Boston Public Library, 1982.

T

Tappert, Tara Leigh. *Cecilia Beaux and the Art of Portraiture*. Washington: Smithsonian Institution Press, 1995.

Theresa Bernstein: An Early Modernist. New York: Joan Whalen Fine Art, 2000.

Theresa Bernstein: Expressions of Cape Ann & New York, 1914 – 1972. Stamford Museum & Nature Center, 1990.

Troyen, Carol. *The Boston Tradition*. Boston: Museum of Fine Arts, 1980.

Truettner, William H., and Roger B. Stein, eds. *Picturing Old New England : Image and Memory*. New Haven: Yale University Press, 1999.

Tufts, Eleanor. *American Women Artists*. Washington: National Museum of Women in the Arts, 1987.

Tysver, Ted. "A Survey of the North Shore Arts Association." *American Art Review*. Aug 1997: 120-125.

V

Vose, Robert C. *The Return of William Morris Hunt* . Boston: Vose Galleries, Inc., 1986.

W

Waldren, Joy. "Paul Strisik." *Southwest Art*. June 1991: 62 – 67.

Ward, Meredith. *Adventure & Inspiration*. New York: Hirschl & Adler Galleries, 1988.

Warren, Jill. "A Candid Conversation with Paul Strisik." *Art West*. Jan/Feb 1983, Vol. VI, Issue 2, 68 – 75.

Whipple, Barbara. "The Eloquence of Cecilia Beaux." *American Artist*. Sept 1974: 45-51.

Willard Metcalf: An American Impressionist. Exhibition Catalogue. New York: Spanierman Gallery, 1996.

William Lamb Picknell, 1853 – 1897. Washington D.C.: Taggart & Jorgenson Gallery, 1991.

Wilmerding, John. *Paintings by Fitz Hugh Lane*. New York: Harry N. Abrams, Inc., 1988.

---, *Audubon, Homer, Whistler and Nineteenth Century America* . New York: The McCall Pub. Co., 1970.

---, *Fitz Hugh Lane*. New York: Praeger Pub., 1971.

Winslow Homer: A Selection from the Cooper-Hewitt Collection, Smithsonian. Washington: Smithsonian Institution Press, 1972.

Winslow Homer. Exhibition Catalogue. New York: Spanierman Galleries, 1966.

Winslow Homer. Exhibition Catalogue. Tucson: University of Arizona, 1963.

Worley, Sharon. "Max Kuehne." *American Art Review*. Oct 1997: 124-131.

Wright, John Hardy. *Images of America: Gloucester and Rockport* . Charleston: Arcadia Pub., 2000.

Z

Zabel, Barbara. *Selections from the Edgemarle Collection American Women Artists 1860 – 1960*. Old Lyme: Lyme Academy Gallery, 1987.

Zellman, Michael David., ed. *American Art Analog*. 3 vols. New York: Chelsea House Publishers, 1986.

ACKNOWLEDGMENTS

MANY PEOPLE have been instrumental in the production of this book, providing information or access to research materials and images. I am very thankful for having had the opportunity to write this book and for the cooperation from so many galleries, museums, private collectors and the team that collaborated to plan the project.

THE TEAM

Ann Fisk. Former Director of the Rockport Art Association, for her organizational support, and her intimate knowledge of Cape Ann and the artists.

Tom Nicholas N.A. For his exceptional skills as an artist and his uncanny eye in evaluating paintings for inclusion in the book... and for being my Godfather.

Bill Trayes. For his encyclopedic knowledge of the history and art of Cape Ann.

Thomas Davies. For his 35 years of experience and knowledge of Cape Ann art and his tireless efforts in obtaining images for the book, a majority of which are included due to his efforts.

Private Collectors. Thanks to the many private collectors who graciously lent their pictures for inclusion in the book.

Cape Ann. Thanks to the many local organizations and institutions on Cape Ann for allowing us to reproduce work from their collections: Rockport Art Association, the Town of Rockport, the Rockport National Bank, and The Seaward Inn.

Galleries. Thanks to the numerous galleries and their staffs that provided support for the project, lending transparencies and obtaining permission from owners to reproduce their works of art. A special thanks is extended to Terry Vose for his time, enthusiasm and invaluable help in locating several important works for the book.

Adelson Galleries, Inc.
A.J. Kollar Fine Paintings
Alfred J. Walker Fine Art
Babcock Gallery
Brown Corbin Fine Art
Curtis Galleries

David Findlay Jr. Fine Art, NYC
David Hall Fine Works of Art and Appraisal
Davies Fine Arts
DeVille Galleries
Gerald Peters Gallery
Godel & Co. Fine Art
Goldfield Galleries
Greenwich Gallery
Hirschl & Adler Galleries
Keny Galleries
Kenneth Lux Gallery
Mark LaSalle Fine Arts
McClees Galleries
R.H. Love Galleries
Royal Galleries
Salander O'Reilly Galleries
Shannon Fine Art Auctioneers
Sotheby's, Inc.
Spanierman Gallery LLC.
The Caldwell Gallery
The Cooley Gallery
The Schwarz Gallery
Vaga Visual Arts & Galleries Inc.
Vance Jordan Fine Art
Vose Galleries of Boston

Museums. Thanks to the following museums for their contributions.

Addison Gallery of American Art, Philips Academy
Canajoharie Library and Art Gallery
Cape Ann Historical Association
Mead Art Museum
Museum of Fine Arts, Boston
National Gallery of Art
Smithsonian American Art Museum
The Peabody Essex Museum
Sandy Bay Historical Society and Museums
Westmoreland Museum of American Art
William Lamb Picknell Catalogue Raisonne Project